"Human Action comes from human motivation… human thought. So that is the Power of Happy Thoughts. These are very right words. Many problems today exist because of negligence of inner peace. So, first create inner peace through Happy Thoughts, which shall then even guide science and technology in the external world."

~His Holiness the Dalai Lama, while releasing Sirshree's book, "The Warrior's Mirror" in 10 languages

Many books talk about having the right thoughts, but don't show you how. The uniqueness of the book The Source is that it shows you how to create the right thoughts from inside. The second unique quality of this book is that it shows exactly how to handle the negativities around us by tapping the source within.

~Shahrukh Khan, while releasing Sirshree's book, "The Source"

"Friends and colleagues in the field of Yoga, this book which I have read, is no doubt a guide for you. I appreciate the book and I think each and every one should have it in their hands. And when there's friction, you can go through it, so that your mind develops the qualities of quietness and peace."

~Dr. B.K.S. Iyengar while releasing Sirshree's book, "Complete Meditation"

This book explains how a happy natural state paves the way for everything you desire in life – with, of course, a little help from 'the one above'. As the author, Sirshree observes, There is no way to happiness; happiness itself is the way.

~Dr. Vijay Bhatkar, Ph.D., scientist and innovator on Sirshree's book, "The One Above"

The Source is an admirable book. It contains a large number of examples which Sirshree gives from daily life as well as questions and answers. Efforts of this nature (publishing the book) is important and I wish it was done on a much larger scale using technology so that value systems are understood since it is these values that are ultimately the base of all religion. The base of all religion is not theology or philosophy or the outer aspect of rituals; what really matters is that the thought behind all these should be Happy Thoughts.

~Prof M.G.K. Menon, renowned scientist, while releasing Sirshree's book, "The Source"

In every word of Sirshree, there is love. His knowledge is full of love.

~Anup Jalota, Singer, while releasing Sirshree's book, "The Magic of Awakening"

the Source™

Power of Happy Thoughts

SIRSHREE

The Source... Power of Happy Thoughts
By Sirshree Tejparkhi

ISBN : 978-93-87696-05-1

Published by WOW Publishings Pvt. Ltd., India

First edition published in November 2011
Third edition published in April 2018
Fourth edition published in January 2020

To the great seers and thinkers
who discovered the laws of the mind and beyond,
that every era shall continue to benefit from.

Contents

Part II – Powers of the Source

Part III – Living with the Source

Preface

We all go through such phases in life when we live by unconsciously choosing to be victims to limitations that we experience. Many of us tend to be consumed with physical ailments, instability in relationships, frustrations at the workplace, emotional fragility, and financial insecurity which cause us to feel victimized.

But what if you came to know that life is not something that happens *to us*; rather, it is something that happens ***through*** us!

Through us?! You may ask. If life is happening *through* us, from where does it originate? Where do thoughts originate? What causes the first thought when we wake up in the morning? What is the source of thoughts? And what is the ultimate source of everything? What is the real purpose of creation of this world?

Every day, you engage in the world and operate through your thoughts, your feelings, the words that you speak or write, and resultant actions. You have been operating in the dimension of thoughts and feelings.

You're about to discover the origin of all these – the Source!

The experience of the Source harmonizes the quest for inner peace with the pursuit for success in the external world. You can indeed experience both! You can effortlessly progress towards your highest potential while you revel in unbroken peace, permanent happiness, and unconditional love of the Source.

The Source, which is the foundation of thought and feeling, does not belong in the realm of mind. It is beyond the mind.

Due to the popular wave of manifestation techniques, many of us are led to believe that thoughts are the key to creating a life filled with health, wealth and harmony in relationships.

Discussions on the law of attraction and manifestation fall short of explaining the deeper nuances of life. They do not give satisfactory answers to how we can experience a life of permanent and boundless bliss. Many have attempted and claimed that the positive-thinking paradigm does not help to fully account for the unexplainable predicaments that arise in life.

Being able to manifest what you desire does not necessarily guarantee lasting happiness. This is the missing link in the practice of manifestation techniques based on the law of attraction. Without understanding this missing link, it is common for people to get into frenzy with manifesting their desires by using the power of thoughts, believing that it would deliver lasting happiness.

Since thoughts are used as the key to manifesting what we desire in life, we rarely get the thought of unlocking this key! This book provides the key to unlock the secret behind our thoughts; it is an invitation to access the Source of all creation.

Those who have been able to unlock the secret of thoughts have attained the ultimate treasure of life. They have reveled in the experience of boundless bliss, unconditional love, and unbroken peace. They have expressed the highest creation of life.

The only way to experience true and lasting love, joy and peace is to abide in the Source of everything. Accessing the Source is the key to the ultimate treasure of life – a treasure that is already present within you.

Part I of the book, 'The Wisdom of the Source', provides insights to the experience of the Source. You will discover the way to connect with the Source within you and to dwell in the state of unbroken bliss.

What is the Source? How can it be accessed? What are the roadblocks in accessing and abiding in the Source?

This section provides answers to these profound questions and explains what it means to experience the living presence of the Source. The associated meditations lead you beyond the realm of thinking in the direct experience of the Source.

Part II, 'The Powers of the Source', is about the quest for inner peace. It expounds seven powerful attributes of the Source. Each attribute unravels a key facet, which is not only the expression of the Source, but also a gateway to access and abide in it.

Each power brings to light aspects of stilling the mind by going beyond thoughts. These Powers are ways of abiding in a happy natural state, conducive for creation from the Source. The direct experience of the Source brings loving acceptance and peace. It expresses as causeless happiness, patience, and detached passion. You can naturally progress toward your highest potential when you express these qualities by abiding in the experience of the Source.

Part III, 'Living with the Source' is about the pursuit for worldly success. It helps you fill the missing pieces in the jigsaw puzzle of creating a perfect life. It directs you to attain the inner state of bliss from where creation happens effortlessly so that a life of abundance, vitality and harmony can be achieved.

This section explains seven laws of the mental realm that serve to guide our thoughts and feelings by harnessing the powers of the Source. It explains how you can successfully function in the world by abiding in the Source. Understanding the principles of thinking can help to neutralize negativity and channel our thoughts towards realizing our highest potential..

Imagine life as a movie. The movie could be a success story, a story of love, a comedy, an adventure, or a tragedy. Or perhaps it could be a mix of two or more genres.

What if we were to awaken one day and realize that we are the writer, the editor, the protagonist, the producer, the director, the hero, the villain, and also the audience of our own movie?! What if we learned to playfully enact this drama of life by reveling in the experience of the Source?

This book is about opening up to these possibilities. It serves as a doorway to a life filled with love, bliss and creativity, to a new you!

Part I

The Wisdom of the Source

1

Quest for Love, Joy and Peace
Where can it be found?

There was a Sufi mystic called Rabiya. She was renowned for her deep insights on human life and divinity.

One evening, she was searching for something on the street outside her hut. The sun was setting and it was getting dark as few people gathered around her. "What are you searching for? Perhaps we can help," they told Rabiya.

Rabiya said, "I have lost my needle."

One amongst the people said, "The sun is setting and it will be very difficult to find the needle in the dark. If you tell us where it had fallen, it will be easier to find it."

Rabiya told them, "Actually it has not fallen on this road. It has fallen inside my house."

Everyone started laughing. Then one of them said, "If the needle has fallen inside your house, then why are you searching here on the road!?"

Rabiya replied, "There is no light inside the house. There is still some light here. So I thought of searching here."

Somebody said, "Even if there is light, how can we find the needle here if it has not been lost here? It makes sense in bringing light inside your house, so that you can find the needle."

Rabia laughed, "Indeed! This common sense prevails for trivial matters in the outside world. When are you going to apply this common sense to your inner life? You crave love from people; you yearn for happiness in pleasures of the senses; you seek peace by changing your surroundings. Does it make sense in searching outside all your life, when it has been lost within you!?"

Rabia returned home, leaving the people awestruck.

Love, Happiness and Peace have always been present within each one of us. It's just that we seldom notice and experience them.

When people lose the experience of true happiness within them, their pursuit turns outward in the material world. Satisfaction in external pursuits is instant, but temporary.

The home consumer products industry exploits this human condition to their advantage. They sell products that people don't really need by convincing them that it will enhance their sense of fulfillment. For example, if you use this particular bath soap, you will appear more beautiful, happy and lively. They set standards for beauty by portraying celebrities who vouch for their products.

Indirectly, they create fixations in people's minds about what will give them greater fulfillment. Use a particular brand of clothes and you will stand out in the crowd. Thus our true identity is invested in brands! Love, happiness and peace, which are qualities of who we truly are within, are invested in things of the outside world.

Trying to find true fulfillment in external things doesn't work. In the insatiable quest to amass more and better comforts, people lose their value for true love, bliss and peace. It leaves them hungry for more and so they remain dissatisfied all the time.

It is like trying to catch the head of your shadow. It always eludes you. Catch hold of your head itself, and the shadow is automatically caught!

When you seek true love, happiness and peace within, you discover that their source is within you.

What you were seeking outside is like a shadow. It can never give lasting fulfillment. Your outer world only reflects your inner world. When you connect to the Source of life within and abide in its experience, your life automatically reflects it through the expression of love, bliss and peace in the external world.

During childhood, we would have been told what we should be doing and what we shouldn't. We have observed the behaviors of our parents, neighbors, school teachers and unconsciously borrowed our perspectives about life.

We would have observed and learned the values that people uphold and things that people pursue in their lives. It is true that what we pursue in life personally is largely determined by what we have learned from the world around us.

Instead of seeking what we really want in life, we tend to align with standards that our social setup determines for us. Our desires have become so superficial that we have stopped questioning what truly gives us lasting fulfillment.

Let us examine what every human being really wants through some examples:

> When a young man was asked what he wants, he said, "I want a good smartphone."
>
> He was then asked, "Why do you want a smartphone?"
>
> He replied, "So that I can connect with my friends and family; so that I can get my tasks done."
>
> Further, he was asked, "Why do you want to connect with friends and family? What do you gain through them?"
>
> He thought about it and then said, "I get happiness."
>
> Another person was asked the same question, he said, "I want to put an end to the daily arguments that I have with my wife."
>
> "Why do you want to put an end to it?"
>
> "I wish that it ends so that my marriage improves."
>
> "What will you gain by improving your relationship?"
>
> He thought over this and replied, "Love."
>
> When someone else was asked what he wants, he answered, "I wish that the children in my neighbourhood stop playing in the common area after 8 in the evening."
>
> "Why shouldn't they play after 8?"

"Then I won't be troubled by the noise and commotion that they create."

"What will you gain with this?"

He replied, "I will be at peace."

We can see from these examples that all our desires finally amount to experiencing love, happiness and peace.

Try this out with yourself. Take a pause for a minute and introspect, 'What is it I really want?' Randomly choose any one wish that you have and ask, "Why do I want this wish to be fulfilled? What do I really want from it?"

When you repeatedly question yourself this way, it will finally lead you to your true yearning for Love, Happiness or Peace.

When you clearly understand what you are actually looking for through all your endeavors, then you can steer your seeking in a unified direction – Love, Happiness and Peace. This is the real desire of every human being.

The truth is that Love, Joy and Peace are the ultimate goal of everyone's life. Why, then do people still remain deprived of true happiness and suffer all their lives? The reason is quite simple; people are not clear about what they truly want and where they can find it.

The chapters that follow in this part of the book lead you through the journey of connecting and abiding in the experience of the Source.

Being in the experience of the Source automatically reflects through positive expressions of health, wealth, loving relationships, abundance, creativity, compassion, simplicity and ease in life.

2

Watching your thoughts
How to access the Source?

A disciple once asked his master, "O Holy master, please tell me, in one sentence, what the essence of religion is."

The master replied, "I will tell you in one word."

The disciple was curious, "Please impart that one word to me."

The master calmly replied, "Silence."

Eagerly, the disciple asked, "How does one attain this silence?"

"By meditating," the wise one replied.

"How should we meditate?" asked the disciple.

The master smiled, "By being in silence."

Silence is the way and also end in itself. This Silence is not the absence of sound, conversation or thoughts. It is the basis of life itself. It is the Source of all expression.

Before we look at what the Source essentially is, let us first get a first-hand experience within us. It is possible to experience it, even before understanding it, because the experience of the Source is present constantly within each of us.

Once you experience it, understanding it will probably be easier. Let us now perform a short exercise to experience a glimpse of this inner silence.

Watching your thoughts – the Thought numbering meditation

Here is a powerful meditation to help you access the inner silence. Consider spending five minutes actually practicing it after reading the instructions that follow.

Though the meditation may seem very simple, it is pivotal in gaining an experiential shift in your understanding about thoughts. This meditation is one of the ways of actually accessing the Source. We will see many more as we read further.

In this short meditation, you will attempt to give a number to every thought. Do not begin the meditation yet. Understand the instructions first.

It is advisable to set a timer for five minutes. Use your cell phone, or your computer or a clock timer to set an alarm only for five minutes.

In this meditation, as soon as a thought arises, you will give it a number. Begin with the number 1. Wait for the next thought to arise. You will then count 2.

Watch, as your thoughts come and go and let them continue in a normal, natural manner. Some thoughts may be positive, some negative, some related to work, while others may be thoughts of boredom. Whatever be the thought, count them regardless of the type of thought that arises.

You may get thoughts regarding this meditation itself, "What is the use of this meditation?"or "This does not seem to help." Just give a number to each such thought as well and then await the next thought.

Your mind might wander away and pursue a trail of thoughts instead of numbering. If this happens, whenever you remember, start from '1' all over again.

Continue this meditation till the timer goes off.

Having understood the instructions, practice it. It just takes five minutes. All that it takes is to watch your thoughts, number them and let them pass. Keep counting up with every passing thought. If you forget the count, start from 1 all over again. So, go on and do it. You will be able to answer the questions that follow only if you have practiced it.

Now, if you have indeed spent five minutes practicing this meditation, here are three simple questions for you to consider.

Was there a gap between thoughts?

Were there moments when there were no thoughts?

Were there moments when you were waiting for a thought?

You may have answered "yes" to one of these questions. In all probability, you would have answered yes to at least two of the three questions. This sets the context for understanding what the Source is.

If the answer to any of these questions in your experience is "yes", what was that state? It was certainly not the mind. The mind is nothing but thoughts. You use your mind only when you think on any subject. When you experienced a gap in your thoughts, even if it was for a brief moment, or when you were waiting for thoughts, what was that state? Some may call it an experience of blankness, while some call it a hazy state, and some others call it stillness.

Whatever you call it, you were actually getting a glimpse of the Source of everything. The Source is the wellspring from where thoughts arise.

If not in this meditation, there may have been other instances where a state of nothingness may have been experienced. It may have been while practicing some other meditation, or spontaneous moments when you felt a sense of oneness with everything, perhaps on a nature trail. There may have been moments when your mind was stilled and did not have thoughts, even if they were momentary. These are glimpses of the experience of the Source.

The purpose here is not to use esoteric words like God or Soul. Any word will do. We are calling it the Source, so that it helps us to approach the essence of the experience by avoiding preconceived notions that are associated with known words.

When one reads this, one may say, "So, the Source is a meditative state." The word meditation is often misunderstood. There are exercises that relax the mind. We are not referring to meditations that relax the mind as the experience of the Source.

There are mindfulness exercises such as focusing your attention on the breath or the activities of your body that improves your ability to concentrate and be in the present. Again, we are not referring to meditations that help concentrate as the experience of the Source.

There are other exercises where you pray or chant or visualize by holding onto intentions. We are not referring to meditations that focus on intentions as the experience of the Source.

Through some of these exercises, it is possible that you may attain a thoughtless state. The experience that exists in a thoughtless state is the experience of the Source. However, this does not mean that the Source cannot be experienced in the presence of thoughts. We shall understand this further.

There are exercises, which can be referred to as consciousness-meditations that can easily help in accessing the Source. Some of these do not even need you to close your eyes. Meditation is not a chore to be practiced once or twice a day. It is a state of being that you can dwell in, whilst going through your daily activities.

In the chapters that follow, as we dwell more on what the Source is, more consciousness-meditations are provided. These are simple exercises that you can practice to access and dwell in the Source.

3

Beyond the mind
What is the Source?

In the kingdom of Mithila ruled the wise King Janaka.

One night, the king had a vivid dream. He was fighting a war and his army was vanquished; he fled from the battlefield.

Running through the jungle for hours, he was exhausted and hungry. He found some food and was about to eat it when a wild boar charged at him, screaming and gnawing at him.

King Janaka cried in pain. He could not take it any more... and he woke up! To his surprise, he found himself resting in comfort in his royal bed in the palace.

For the king, everything had become questionable. "Was that a dream, or is this a dream?" He wondered, "Is it possible that I am actually starving in the jungle after fleeing from battle, and dreaming that I am enjoying the luxuries of this palace? What is the reality?"

He consulted his advisors, the learned pundits of his kingdom, but none could provide a satisfactory answer. Finally, Sage Ashtavakra visited the royal palace when he found that many pundits were being put to trial.

He revealed the truth of existence, "O Rajarishi… Few are those fortunate ones who live in luxuries and yet ponder the profound truth of life… You are a king and also a Rishi (one who grasps the secret of life). This question that has gripped you is auspicious… Many would laugh this away, but few will be able to discern the depth of this question…"

The sage paused and then continued, "Neither this, nor that is real. Both are dreams, both are changing. That which you truly are is permanent, all-pervading, alive and conscious. It is the source of everything. Everything else is temporary, limited and unreal. Experiencing this reality dispels all doubts and gives lasting peace and bliss. Dwelling in doubts and trying to reason only raises more doubts and causes restlessness."

As a human being, you are constantly in one of three states: waking, dream, or deep (dreamless) sleep. In the waking state, you perceive the world through your senses – sights through the eyes, sounds through the ears, smells and tastes through the nose and tongue, touch through the skin.

However the world that we perceive as our reality is only a partial reality. The risk of being limited to awareness of this partial reality is that we begin to judge and assume the complete reality on the basis of whatever we perceive through our senses. The world of senses is made the reference to infer the complete reality.

However, the truth is that our sense perceptions constitute a derived reality – a reality that is projected by the mind based on sense perceptions.

The mind is a derived existence in itself. It is borne out of a bundle of thoughts that project an individual identity. But what is the source of the mind? From where do thoughts emerge? When we experience the source of the mind, the complete reality is revealed. The Source is the living essence that exists beyond the mind, beyond the states of waking, dream and deep sleep.

What is it that enables your eyes to see? What is the light that enables us to see not just light, but also darkness? We may call it the Source, Consciousness, God or Self. It is the same life principle that pervades everyone and everything. It is the reason we are alive.

The Source is beyond the concepts of time and space. It is an undifferentiated state of wholeness beyond duality. Its nature is pure existence, which is aware of itself through the medium of the manifest world.

The expression of the world appears like waves on the surface of the ocean of pure silence. Pure silence is the core of existence. It is beyond the duality of sound and relative silence (which is merely the absence of sound). All forms and phenomena arise and dissolve in this eternal silence.

The Source pervades all manifestation. It is the screen of consciousness on which the movie of life is being projected. This screen is the creator, the projector, the essence, and also the experiencer of the movie of life.

Awareness is the essential principle of the Source. Pure awareness, or pure wakefulness, brings about the manifestation of forms and phenomena. Our mind, comprising thoughts and feelings, is the expression of pure awareness. Our body is a dense, more obvious expression of the Source, a gross expression of the mind.

The human body-mind is a medium through which the Source experiences itself and expresses its divine qualities.

It is only due to the presence of consciousness–the knowing principle–that your eyes can see, that your ears can hear. Its presence enlivens your tongue to speak. And yes, it is due to its presence that thoughts arise.

While thinking and doing are the key aspects of thoughts, *Being* is the essence of the Source. *Beingness* is the experience of existence; it is the "is-ness" of life. It's that feeling of being awake and alive, within which everything is being manifested. This experience of presence or aliveness is constantly happening within every human being.

The Source cannot be understood as one would any other subject, as it is beyond concepts, beyond the comprehension of the intellect. While it may defy explanation for many, there is no denying its existence – for it is existence itself!

When you learn that the experience of the Source is constantly going on within each of us, you might imagine that this entity exists within the human body. And, though it may be considered true logically, the Source is not just within the body. Rather, the body exists within the Source. All of this existence is happening within the Source.

Think of a fish living in water. Water is an all-pervading presence for the fish. It is the essential medium that keeps the fish alive. Water exists not only within the fish, but also all around it. Water is so close to its eyes that the fish doesn't realize that it's in water. What if the fish swam off in search of water, asking, "Where is water?"

This is precisely what the questioning mind would ask when it is told about the all-pervading nature of consciousness: "Where is this consciousness? Is it within me, or elsewhere?"

The experience of presence or consciousness is so close to you; in fact, it is your very essence. If you carefully observe, you will find that the spatial concepts of *within* and *outside* are relative to your body and belong in the realm of thoughts. From the standpoint of the Source, there is neither a *within* nor an *outside*. You are *presence*. Your presence is the experience of the Source.

When an individual identity is assumed in thoughts, it gives birth to the notion of a separate 'I', confined within the boundaries of the human body. With the birth of this illusory separate 'I', whatever happens with the body-mind, seems to happen to a 'me', whatever belongs at the body-level becomes 'mine'.

Whatever is inside the skin is 'me' and everything else outside is 'not me'. We have been living this myth without questioning it, because we find everyone else around us living with the same illusion.

This illusion is complete when the flip-side of "I... me... mine" is also *imagined* into existence. Whatever is 'not me' is perceived as 'you... we... they... it'. This illusion is the root cause of all suffering, struggle and various defilements such as fear, anger, hatred, ill-will, and jealousy.

Forgetfulness of who we truly are leads to false identification with who we are not. We have become so addicted to the beliefs and stories that constitute our false personality that we continually try to improve and enrich this personality.

In the competitive world, personality is often used as a mask to flaunt who we are as individuals. But it is actually a superficial outfit that can be changed. Working on personality doesn't cause any harm unless we believe that we *are* the personality. It is not difficult to notice that no matter how much we work on our personality, we lack the fulfillment of who we truly are.

True fulfillment is experienced when we dwell in the essence of who we truly are.

The Source is from where thoughts originate. Thinking about the experience of the Source has nothing to do with actually experiencing it. Thoughts have nothing to do with *being*. To experience and create from the Source, we need to transcend thoughts.

One may say, "I can feel the presence of the Source." Another may say, "The experience of the Source is blissful." and yet another may say, "The Source cannot be described." These statements have nothing to do with the real experience of the Source. These are mere qualifying statements that arise as thoughts – and thoughts can never define the Source. The most we can do is to point to the Source.

A young child once asked his father what the colour green looked like. The father, whose finger was stained with red ink, pointed the stained finger in the direction of a tree and said, "That's green." The child, instead of looking at the tree beyond the two of them, fixed his gaze on his father's stained finger and said, "Yes. I understand."

You can see that he has mistaken the red stain on his father's finger to be green. The child then carries this misunderstanding with him throughout his life after mistaking the colour of the pointing finger to be the colour of what was being pointed at.

In the same way, people may spend their lifetime imprisoned within the limitations of thoughts and yet, they may claim to have experienced the Source. But, like the young child in this example, they really do not truly know it through direct experience.

The Source has been pointed at in various ways. Many who have realized the Source have written, spoken, and sung about it. But all these forms of expression are merely pointers, nothing more than stained fingers! Far too many individuals spend their lives paying attention to the pointers instead of to what they are pointing. They argue about them all through their lives; they never look beyond these pointers to what they are pointing to.

Pointers belong in the realm of thoughts. When you look past these pointers and experience consciousness, you experience freedom from the shackles of concepts. Qualities of consciousness such as love, joy, peace, and creativity express freely from this state of freedom .

The highest function of thoughts is to serve as a mirror for pure consciousness to experience itself. The realm of thoughts is your gateway to the Source. When thoughts cease to pull attention, the stillness behind thoughts is revealed. The Source becomes self-aware. The Source returns onto itself.

However, thoughts do not serve this purpose due to the habit of compulsive thinking. Compulsive thinking is a disease that plagues most people in varying degree. This is caused by the habit of being attached to the content of thoughts. We're attracted to information held within our thoughts.

Consider this: we rarely look at thoughts as they are. We tend to indulge in thoughts by attaching our personalized meanings to them. We fall into a trap when we associate feelings with the content of our thoughts. If we have to move from where we are today toward accessing the Source, we then need to understand effective ways to break our attachment to thoughts.

Let us consider another meditation to access the Source and experience freedom.

Detaching from your thoughts – the 'Next' meditation

The practice of meditation is an effective way of detaching from thoughts and feelings that pull your attention. However, when people sit in meditation, they are often overcome by a deluge of thoughts. People are unable to break out of the habit of compulsive thinking. They are unable to detach from thoughts and feelings. This leads to a constant feeling of discontentment and incompleteness within.

The key purpose of this exercise is to de-focus from the content of thoughts by letting them pass by and saying "Next." This way, you allow thoughts to pass by so that they do not hold your attention.

Close your eyes and watch your thoughts as they pass by.

Don't judge them. Simply observe them as they continually pass by. Watch as thoughts come and go. Allow this to occur. Let them continue in a normal, natural manner.

Some thoughts may be positive, some negative, some may be related to your work, while others may surface without context. Keep your body steady regardless of the type of thoughts that arise.

Watch the thought, let it pass without chasing it, and silently utter the word "Next." The word "Next" acts as an anchor, allowing thoughts to reach their natural conclusion and dissolve.

Saying "Next" also raises your awareness of the gap between the thought that's receding and the next thought that's appearing. This interval may be as momentary as a thousandth of a second, but focus on that point regardless of the length of time.

In that interval there is no thought . . . everything has stopped and is frozen in that moment. In this gap, you begin to experience the silence which is the background of thoughts.

When you're watching a passing train from the railway platform, you catch a glimpse of the opposite platform in the gaps between two cars. In the same way, you glimpse the silence presence in the gap between two thoughts.

You don't need to be worried if you miss the gap; instead, simply pay attention to the next thought and allow it to pass.

When you meditate but don't see any immediate results, you may become disappointed. The mind, in turn, may respond through an inability to concentrate. Focusing on thoughts of disappointment, though, will only drain your energy.

Remember: The goal is not a tangible result. The actual purpose is to become aware of the presence of the Source by being in the gap between thoughts.

The key is to just watch these thoughts as if they were dark clouds passing by, momentarily shrouding the sunlight – clouds that are far away, that don't affect you. Observe these thoughts with a detached feeling, as if you are a "witness" watching them from afar.

When thoughts of disappointment occur, never say, "I am disappointed." You are not your emotions; you are experiencing them. Instead, say, "Thoughts of disappointment are passing through my awareness." Simply dismiss them by saying "Next" and moving on to watch the next one.

Similarly, when you feel boredom, never say, "I am bored." Instead, say, "Thoughts of boredom are passing through my awareness." Allow them to pass by saying "Next".

This is one of the most powerful and, surprisingly, easiest ways to access the Source. If done properly, it takes just a few moments. After some practice, you'll be able to access the Source with the help of this exercise. Why don't you try it now?

Detaching from your thoughts helps in accessing and abiding in the Source. The more you practice this, you will find that old thoughts that used to cling and plague your awareness die down and are replaced by an entirely new set of thoughts, arising from the Source.

As you practice this and other meditations explained in this book, you will discover the Source through experience. The distinction that the Source is consciousness, the Self that is knowing (and hence distinct from) thoughts will become clear.

4

Finding who you are *not*

Who accesses the Source?

There lived a couple in a village. One fine day, Uncle John visited them. The husband was at work. Uncle John approached the wife and said, "I am Uncle John."

Assuming that he must be her husband's uncle, the wife welcomed Uncle John and made him comfortable. She served him food and then made a call to her husband to inform that Uncle John had come.

Her husband assumed that he might be her uncle. After reaching home, he met Uncle John and directly started conversing with him. By now, the wife became sure that he was her husband's uncle.

Uncle John mingled with the family so easily that they received him with unquestioning faith and hospitality. No one ever questioned his credentials. They treated him with affection and respect.

Uncle John continued his stay at their house for many days and started raising his demands for delicacies to be served to his taste.

One day, the troubled man asked his wife, "When is your uncle going to leave? Had he not been your uncle, I wouldn't have tolerated him." His wife was startled, "My uncle!? I thought he's your uncle. For all these days, I have worked hard to make him comfortable."

The truth suddenly dawned on both of them. As soon as they realized that Uncle John was an impostor masquerading as their relative, he vanished from the scene!

The 'I' that each of us uses to refer to our individual selves is similar to Uncle John. It resides within you as long as you don't question its credentials. The moment you begin to doubt the authenticity of the 'I', it begins to dissolve, revealing the experience of the Source.

The mind is a bundle of thoughts in which each thought is linked to a point of reference – the 'I'. This point of reference called 'I' is a false notion that keeps changing every instant.

The following example will clarify how the reference of 'I' keeps changing. Consider the following sentences that one commonly speaks.

> My hand was wounded when I had been to the workshop.
>
> I was scared when I found that my hand was bleeding profusely.
>
> I then thought of visiting the doctor to dress up the wound.

When one says, "*I had been to the workshop*", the word 'I' is being used to refer to the body. You keep saying many such things during the day by assuming yourself as the body. *I had food, I climbed the stairs, I laughed* etc. Here 'I' refers to the body.

The same sentence also says, '*My hand was wounded*'. Whom does the 'My' refer to? If the earlier identification with the body were to be used, one would have said, "I was wounded." When you say, 'My hand was wounded', you consider yourself the owner of your body. It is only when you assume yourself to be separate from the body that you can say '*My* hand'. Thus, the point of reference for the 'I' has shifted from the body to the owner of the body in the same sentence.

When you say, "*I was scared*", the 'I' in this context refers to the mind. The body cannot feel scared. The mind feels scared just as it also feels sad or elated, moody or ecstatic.

"*I thought of visiting the doctor*." Here again, the reference has shifted from the mind to the intellect. Thinking is considered an intellectual faculty. Here you assume yourself to be the intellect.

From this example, you can understand how the point of reference is false and also how it keeps changing. The use of the words 'I', 'Me', 'Mine' differs in various contexts. This was an example of only three sentences.

Upon deeper reflection, you will come across innumerable identities of 'I'. Different identities of 'I' spring into awareness at different points in time. However, due to delusion, you always believe it to be the same 'I'. Being lost in this delusion, the real 'I' remains in the dark. Your true nature never gets an opportunity to shine forth as it is eclipsed by these false identities.

Introspecting the 'I'

Asking yourself, "Who am I now?" is one of the most powerful ways of breaking out of this identification with the false 'I'. When you ask this question relentlessly, it leads you inevitably to the experience of the Source.

The 'I' thought is the root thought, the first thought from which all other thoughts borrow their reference. 'Who am I now?' questions this thought, eventually leading to the fall of the illusory 'I'.

By seeking the masquerading 'I', you will discover that there is nothing that can readily be called the mind. Thoughts gather together, imprint on memory, leading to an impression that the mind exists. When you ask, "Who am I now?" all other thoughts are put to rest. This form of examination puts an end to them with finality. After ending all other identifying thoughts, the question, "Who am I now?" will also dissolve into the stillness of the Source. This is why you can effectively move beyond thoughts by seeking the truth of the 'I' in any situation.

You can begin to use it the moment a stray thought or a negative thought appears – be it of fear, greed, sorrow, rejection, worry, or any other negative expression. Ask yourself: "*To whom has this thought occurred?*" You may also respond to these negative thoughts, depending on the exact one you received, "Who is afraid?" or "Who is feeling rejected?" Your answer will probably be: "Me." Then ask the next question: "But right now, who is this *me*? Where is this '*I*'?" Seek the 'I'. Is it on the body? Is it in thoughts?"

When you introspect in this manner, the thought will dissolve. When the thought dies down, the Source is revealed as the silent stillness in the background. After a few moments, another thought may appear. You'll again ask yourself, "Now to whom has this thought occurred?" The reply will be: "To me." You will once again ask, "Who am I now?"

When the mind drops, the Source is revealed. The Source is always present. Thoughts cloud it. With the practice of meditation, when the mind drops, the Source experiences itself. Consciousness, which was earlier invested in thoughts, becomes aware of its own presence.

The mind that wishes to seek the experience of the Source may keep checking, "Is this the experience of the Source?", "Am I experiencing presence?" This is so subtle that we get identified with the mind and declare, "I cannot experience the Source."

The mind may even take credit by saying, "I experienced the Source;" or "I loved the experience of Presence."

At such junctures, the practice of introspecting the 'I' comes to our aid. Question the thought, "Who is wishing to experience the Source? Who is this 'I' right now?" You will find that the 'I' dissolves into the real silence of the Source.

The highest function of thoughts is to serve as a mirror for pure consciousness to experience itself. The realm of thoughts is your gateway to the Source. When thoughts cease to pull attention, the ever-present stillness behind thoughts is revealed, and the Source becomes self-aware.

Suppose that you are looking at a picture. Now, what if the picture wants to see your eyes?! This sounds absurd. How can the picture see your eyes?! The eyes see the picture and that proves the existence of eyes to the one who is seeing through them.

In the same way, thoughts can never know the Source. The Source is aware of thoughts. However, thoughts indicate the existence of the Source to the Source.

Pointers to get to the root of 'I'

Let us look at points to consider in the practice of dismantling the fallacy of the masquerading 'I':

- When you ask yourself, "Who am I now?" you may tend to answer it intellectually, "I am this," or, "I am not this," from memory. However, whatever you bring from memory is the past. You are interested in knowing "Who am I *right now*?" Hence, you are not meant to answer this question from memory using words. This question compels you to seek the 'I' that is present right now. You go beyond preconceived notions and experience who this 'I' is now pointing at.

- As the practice progresses, the mind may invariably make it a mechanical ritual of providing readymade answers. To break this habit of the mind, try to go deeper into the feeling of curiosity beyond words, even if only for a few seconds. "Who is the one who is asking?" is another effective question that leads you beyond fixed answers.

- The insight that you receive every time you touch the inner stillness is important; not the intellectual answer you may think you have. In fact, 'Who am I now?' is not actually a question. It is a pointer to the one who asks. It needs to be experienced, not answered.

- Whenever a thought arises, you don't need to spend time in contemplating it. Allow the thought to pass as soon as you sense it arising in your mind. At that instant, ask: "To whom has this thought occurred? Where is this thought arising from? If it is arising within 'me', who is this 'I'?"

- If you find this difficult, ask yourself, "Who is finding it difficult?" If the answer "I am finding it difficult" emerges, then ask, "Who is this I?" Practice this relentlessly.

- You might also be tempted to conclude that if you're not having any thoughts, then your mind is empty. This may even ultimately mislead you to believe that if there is nothing in your mind, there's really no point in continuing the meditation. "I am not having a thought" is also a thought. When this thought arises, take a pause and ask "Who is not having any thought?"

- This introspection on the nature of 'I' need not be limited to a meditation session wherein you are seated with closed eyes at a particular place. This is conducive when you are beginning the practice.

    As you progress, though, this introspection can continue even when you're walking, working, or carrying out daily activities. This allows you to access the Source many times during the day. You can continue to question: Who became sad? Who became happy? Who became angry? Every such question will lead you back to the Source.

Introspection on the 'I', when practiced relentlessly with curiosity, dissolves all prejudices and notions that we have so closely held onto. This may give rise to a feeling of discomfort that at the culmination of this seeking, when nothing remains, it would only be a dull void.

Yet, we must continue the process of introspection persistently. When we patiently go through the discomfort of losing the false 'I', we experience the boundless joy of being freed from the prison of individuality.

The dull void that was feared by being a limited individual turns out to be a dynamic stillness which is the source of the vibrant dance of the universe, the very origin of life itself. It is a stillness which gives rise to music and dance, dynamism and creativity.

The blissful experience of the Source is not the opposite of sorrow. It is inclusive of sorrow as well as joy, and it transcends both. You begin to revel in this bliss of being who you truly are – limitless eternal presence, nothing with the potential of everything!

5

Being Who You Truly Are
Why abide in the Source?

A newborn lion cub whose mother lioness was killed in a skirmish was abandoned. The little cub was discovered by a flock of sheep. One of the lambs took pity on the lion-cub and adopted it.

The lion-cub was fed, nurtured and taught the ways of the sheep. The cub grew up in the flock. It learned to graze and feed on grass. The lion-cub would play with the other sheep and bleat just as they did. The cub grew into a full-sized lion. Yet, he continued to bleat and graze meekly, just as his fellow-sheep did. We shall call him the sheep-lion.

One day a huge lion chanced on the flock of sheep. As he attacked the flock, he stopped in his tracks. He was dumbfounded to see the sheep-lion bleating and running for his life. The lion cornered the timid sheep-lion in no time. He roared at the sheep-lion, "Why are you bleating like those timid sheep? You are one of us! You should be fearless and hunt along with us."

The sheep-lion couldn't believe the lion. He continued to tremble and bleat, pleading to be set free. Seeing that the sheep-lion was beyond reasoning, the lion grabbed him by his mane and dragged him to the nearby lake.

The lion thrust the sheep-lion's face above the water and commanded him to look into the water. The sheep-lion leaned over and saw his own reflection for the first time. He was shocked to find that he wasn't a sheep. He was a strong full-grown lion.

The transformation was instant! He roared majestically in delight, having discovered his true identity.

This story shows how we, who are actually the eternal and boundless Source, get confined by the limitations of the body-mind. As a result, we live in fear and dwell in sorrow.

We have seen that the experience of the Source exists beyond thoughts, beyond the false identities that we assume for ourselves.

"But still," you may ask, "what's in it for me? How does accessing the Source really matter? It's fine that I could experience the gap between thoughts… But of what benefit is it to me?"

Again, the question of relevance here is, "Who is this 'I' that you are referring to? What is the real nature of this 'I'?" We have seen that the 'I' that we refer to, keeps changing its reference.

When water occupies a container, it assumes the shape of the container. Though water in essence is formless, when it occupies a glass, it becomes the glass; upon occupying a beaker, it becomes the beaker. In that sense, 'I' is akin to water, since it assumes the form of whatever it gets associated with. By being associated with the body, 'I' becomes the body. By identifying with emotions and thoughts, 'I' becomes the mind and intellect.

In essence, the whole world is a marvelous expression of 'I'. Due to association with everything, the 'I' tends to identify with limited forms, thereby leading to false perception. As a result, we miss the complete reality.

All the parts of a machine, whether small or large, are merely its parts. They do not function for themselves; rather, the machine functions *through* them. If the machine were self-aware, then its parts would also be inherently self-aware.

Due to ignorance, the parts of the machine could feel that they are functioning for themselves and that they have an existence independent of the machine. But they would be mistaken, because you can clearly see the machine functioning as a whole. The parts are merely instrumental for the purpose of the machine. The story of the parts is partial reality. The purpose of the machine is the complete reality.

In the same way, the Source functions through all of us, through our body-mind mechanism. Being ignorant of this, we as human beings assume that we are leading independent, individual lives, separate from the purpose of the 'whole'. Again, this is because we miss the complete reality.

To put things in the right perspective, when we think, breathe, and are self-aware, the Source lives through us. We are no different from the Source.

We consider our bodies to be static entities. If we look deeper, we find that our bodies are actually a dynamic process. They constitute energy that is in continuous flux, taking in carbon, oxygen and other vital elements and disposing of waste. What was tissue in our bodies yesterday is no longer part of those bodies today. Our bodies are being deconstructed and re-engineered every moment as parts of the whole.

When we consider whatever is inside our skin to be "I" and everything that is outside our skin to be "other," we are not recognizing our essential oneness. Accessing and abiding in the Source is about realizing who we truly are; it is about honouring the oneness behind the variety show of the world.

We believe that we are leading life. The truth is that consciousness enlivens this story called 'my life'. This is a paradigm shift in our understanding of our reality.

When we consider ourselves separate from this enlivening principle, we limit ourselves to birth and death. When we become one with life, we allow life to blossom and express through us. Let us allow life to happen, rather than pre-determining criteria about how life should be. This brings us the experience of lasting love, joy and peace, which also spreads its fragrance to those around us.

You may ask, "Does this mean that we should just go with the flow? Then we become like leaves in the wind, swirling here and there?"

Contrary to this, when you realize your oneness with the Source, you attain a state of true freedom. You reach a standpoint where you see the drama of life unfolding and direct life creatively.

When we truly comprehend the grandeur of the Source through direct experience, we gain insight into the infinite potential of the Source that can express through us.

Leading the life of a limited individual without knowing our true nature (the Source) is like a lion mistaking itself to be a sheep. In doing so, we limit the expression of our true potential to miniscule proportions. It is like using the strength of a powerful elephant to hold a matchstick!

In today's increasingly fast-paced world, man experiences a lot of stress, misery, anxiety, demands and struggles. While pursuing happiness and peace, many are not happy or at peace with themselves. By accessing and abiding in the Source, you can let go of all struggle and just dwell in yourself. The most powerful creative potential begins to express itself through you!

Again, you may ask, "Can I be happy by just being myself!?" It is only when you begin to abide in the Source that its wonders will be revealed. You will begin to gain insights that could never be conceived within the limitations of the human intellect.

Great creations are possible when we are rooted in the experience of the Source. This is because the Source expresses through bodies that are receptive, and through which innovations can be manifested. All creative processes are enlivened by pure consciousness and directed by its intelligence. When the awareness of the Source is directed to its own presence, then clarity is experienced. Wholeness and fulfillment are experienced at the deepest level.

The reason the all-pervading consciousness, the Source, cannot unfold its limitless potential through our body-minds is the constant chatter of thoughts, the seemingly endless comparisons, judgments, and negative emotions that plague the mind. Most of us are driven by a deep fear that arises from the sense of separation from totality. Though the experience of the Source is readily available to be accessed, we are not aware of its presence due to the filter of the mind and its conditioning.

When the awareness of the Source is directed towards the seemingly diverse world of forms and phenomena, it gives rise to clouding and confusion. The focus of awareness gets limited and invested into dual opposites such as joy and sorrow, pleasure and pain, life and death, love and hatred, light and darkness.

This loss of self-awareness leads to attachment to the aspects of the manifest world. The wholeness of the Source is shadowed when the mind is absorbed in the objects of perception. As a result of forgetting our essential nature, we begin to cling onto a false idea about our identity; an idea that is implanted by the belief-systems that we inherit through birth and upbringing of the physical body.

We become disconnected from our essential nature. Wholeness– which is our true nature–is lost to us. The nature of wholeness gets fragmented into a perception of limited parts. This fragmentation of wholeness has a ripple effect on well-being at all levels of the human mind-body mechanism – both mental and physical. It leads to emotional imbalance that manifests at the physiological plane as disease.

As infants, we were in the experience of our true nature. We have abided in the bliss of the Source. However, we have shut ourselves out to the experience of pure consciousness by identifying with the chatter of thoughts.

Scientists have conducted experiments on infant brains and found that infant brains have phenomenal adaptability and learning ability due to the fact that they exist in a thoughtless state most of the time. Electro-Encephalogram (EEG) studies have revealed that brain-waves in infants exist in the theta and alpha range, which means very low mental activity. Pure awareness functions without filters in infants. Hence, infants are free from anxiety, stress and depression. Their bodies heal faster and demonstrate immense resilience.

However, if we conduct EEG studies on adults, we find that the constant chatter of the mind shows up as strong beta waves. This is the primary cause of reduced learning abilities as we physically and mentally age. The constant chatter of the mind and deep-set mental conditioning lead to increased probability of stress, anxiety, depression and a general lack of fulfillment, no matter how hard we work to achieve worldly goals.

Meditation practices to access and dwell in the Source lead to reduction in mental clutter, opening the possibility for universal intelligence to function at its highest potential through our body-minds.

Meditation practices can be broadly classified into two types: Attention meditations and Self-awareness meditations.

Attention meditations are exercises of mindfulness where you are focused on what's happening. You are focused on experiences.

Self-awareness meditations are exercises where you are focussed on the experiencer. You use what is being experienced merely as a pretext to be aware of the Presence, which you truly are.

Higher Awareness Leads to Mental Wellbeing

Research has shown that people who practice Self-awareness meditations exhibit significantly improved quotients of creativity, emotional intelligence, creativity and productivity, besides feelings of happiness, empathy and compassion.

The meditations that help access the Source are practices in Self-awareness. They raise the level of awareness of Presence, thereby effecting changes at the emotional and neurological planes.

When you access the Source through the practice of meditation, you are actually loosening the connections of particular neural pathways that trigger the programmed fight-or-flight response in the brain. They also strengthen connections of those neural pathways that are associated with reasoning and higher discrimination.

As a result, when you practice meditation exercises that help in accessing the Source consistently, you gain control of your responses and are able to direct your life situations. Those who do not abide in the experience of the Source through the practice of meditation lead life with a victim mindset, being reactive to life situations.

Healing Intelligence at the Physical Plane

The human immune system comprises trillions of white blood cells and antibodies designed to locate and destroy specific foreign intruders. The body's healing system is a wondrous harmonious orchestra that organizes these lines of defense. The intelligence that functions behind this healing system exists in the wholesome nature of the Source.

True healing is not merely about symptom management; rather it is a transformation that occurs from our original nature of wholeness, from being connected with the Source, directed by the in-built intelligence of the mind-body mechanism. At best, doctors can only facilitate and create conducive conditions at the physiological level for this intelligence to effect healing.

Practice of consciousness meditations which access the Source, have been proven to bring about spontaneous remissions, completely healing terminal diseases like final-stage cancers that were pronounced as incurable.

Being in the experience of the Source is the state of complete liberation from all afflictions of the body-mind. You revel in a state of unconditional happiness, an all-embracing love that is untouched by pleasure or pain, conditional joy or sorrow, attachment or aversion, praise or censure.

Abiding in the experience of the Source has been proven to be the ultimate panacea to imbalances at all levels of human existence. And yet, above all, there is the core truth that makes it obviously natural to return to the Source – *Your very existence is the Source!*

It is then more pertinent to ask – Why *shouldn't* you be yourself!? Be who you truly are. This is the way and also the end in itself!

6

The Hurdles of the Mind

What veils the experience of the Source?

In an office, the boss is working in the cabin and his secretary is seated at her desk outside.

Whenever someone wishes to meet the boss, the secretary goes in to check whether he's available. The secretary has put on a particular perfume that causes the boss to faint at his desk. Seeing that the boss is sleeping at his desk, the secretary comes out and announces that the boss is not available.

This incident keeps repeating. Every time she goes to check whether the boss is available, she finds that he is sleeping. She does not realize that it is her perfume, her presence, which causes the boss to sleep.

When she is informed about the ill-effect of her perfume on the boss, she realizes that whenever she visits the cabin, she will always find the boss asleep. Thereafter, she doesn't feel the need to check on her boss's availability. She unquestioningly announces that the boss is available.

Like the secretary in this story, there is a facet of the mind that poses hurdles in accessing the experience of the Source. It keeps checking in and declaring that the experience of the Source is not available.

Our mind is originally like pure water, which clearly reflects the Presence of the Source. However, it becomes impure when impregnated with thoughts of the individual 'I'. It is these thoughts that are the grime of ego. The intake of impure water is harmful to health. Just as pure water is vital for the health of the body, similarly it is essential to have a pure mind that reflects the Presence of the Source.

All of us have an aspect of mind that can be called the Contrast mind. During infancy, every child abides in the experience of the Source. However, as the child grows, the parental programming and social conditioning lead to the formation of the contrast mind.

The contrast mind is that facet of the mind that discriminates, compares and judges everything. It is the constant chatter that ceaselessly comments about everything that is experienced. Just like the contrast control on a TV remote, which is denoted by a circle with black and white halves, the contrast mind too dwells in duality.

The contrast mind divides everything into silos and labels objects, beings, or circumstances as good or bad, happy or sad, black or white, dark or light, positive or negative, low or high, benefit or loss, and so on. It dwells in fixations of duality. It draws assumptions about everything. Whenever we notice ourselves thinking: "This shouldn't have happened… That should have happened… Why does it always have to be me? Life is so difficult… When will these people change", it is this contrasting aspect of the mind that is at work.

The other facet of the mind is the intuitive mind, which functions spontaneously based on natural intuition and inspiration. Unlike the contrast mind, the intuitive mind is focused on the present task and performs it to the best of its ability. It is free from comparison, judgment, labeling and fixation. Thoughts of the intuitive mind are harmless and constructive.

An example can help understand these facets of the mind.

> When you are scurrying down the stairs, it is the intuitive mind that is functioning. It happens spontaneously and rhythmically.

> However, while going down the stairs, if you get a thought, 'I am climbing down the stairs so well… Uh oh… I only hope I don't trip and fall', this is the contrast mind in action.

> Invariably, when the contrast mind comes in, you may have found that you tend to either miss or jump a step, disturbing the rhythm in which you were climbing down the stairs.

The contrast mind causes us to be stuck in the vicious cycle of polarities such as joy and sorrow, love and hatred. This facet of the mind is caught up in imagined notions, presumptions and beliefs. As a result, it triggers fear, worry, anger and depression. It is this facet of the mind that dwells in past memories or the imaginations and anxieties of the future. Due to this, the present moment is lost to us.

These characteristics of the contrast mind do not allow us to accept the present moment as it is. Non-acceptance of the present moment is the root cause of all sorrow and disease. It is this contrasting nature of the mind that causes disease and depression. It is due to the judging and vacillating nature of the contrast mind that people suffer from insomnia and are forced to consume sleeping pills.

The contrast mind veils the sense of presence. It is like the eclipse that hides the ever-present sun of consciousness. It is a facet of the mind that causes sorrow and disease. Hence it needs to be transcended to restore true happiness, peace and higher consciousness.

Abiding in the Source does not mean that you should be in a thoughtless state. Thoughts of the intuitive mind may continue to occur and enact through the body. To abide in the Source, thoughts of the contrast mind need to be transcended.

The contrast mind poses hurdles in abiding in the Source. There are some major roadblocks that are posed by the contrast mind.

Expectations

The contrast mind tends to make a tangible goal out of everything that is pursued. However, accessing and abiding in the Source is not a tangible goal. It is the enlivening presence in which all pursuits of life are undertaken. Hence, positing a goal and defining expectations cannot lead to the experience of the Source.

Since every external pursuit in life is quantified or qualified in material or tangible terms, the contrast mind tries to set expectations for the purpose of experiencing the Source as well. It will desire to experience such objectives as peace of mind, tranquility, deeper intuition, or greater creativity. If it doesn't immediately see such results, it feels disappointed. It then gives up by assuming that the pursuit is impossible or futile.

The key is to see through all such expectations as the play of the contrast mind. Being the Source is the way and the end in itself. You are already at the destination during the journey. You just need to be present, and allow any such feelings or thoughts of expectations to pass by. Let feelings of disappointment or frustration arise and pass by, for they too are food for the contrast mind.

Boredom

The contrast mind has no role to play when you are in the presence of the Source. As a result, it may cause feelings of boredom. When you are seated in meditation, a few minutes might feel like you've been sitting for an hour. If you are unable to accept this, the meditation may seem difficult to practice and you might even consider giving up.

It's important not to give up at such moments. Continuing to practice being in the stillness of presence despite uncomfortable feelings brings its reward. We shouldn't resist feelings of boredom but rather accept them as a part of the practice. We should continue to watch such feelings as a detached witness. As we persist, such feelings of boredom will pass away, revealing the experience of stillness.

Fixations

Many a times, we may feel we have had a particularly pleasant or unusual spiritual experience. The contrast mind then holds onto this past impression and expects to experience an identical experience again. In doing so, it jumps to conclusions and tries to predetermine the experience of the Source. It constantly compares the present experience with past impressions and causes dissatisfaction. It tries to fix the end result.

We should not be fixated about any one thing. Allow whatever is happening to happen, and let whatever is not happening not happen. We should be intent on experiencing the knower of these fixations. The ultimate purpose is not to know any particular experience we may have, but rather to experience the knower of these experiences.

Blending of the Sense of the body and the Sense of Presence

While practicing Source meditations, the sense of the body serves as a pretext to experience the Sense of Presence. The body sensations – whether painful, pleasurable or neutral – serve as a medium to realize our pure beingness, which is beyond the body.

However, the sense of the body (containing thoughts and feelings) is *not* the Sense of Presence. The sense of the body and the Sense of Presence co-exist and are blended together. This can cause confusion in seeking the experience of the Source.

Two songs are being played simultaneously. We are asked to listen to only one song and not confuse the two together. Initially, we find it difficult, because sometimes our attention goes to one song and sometimes to the other. However, when we train ourselves to attend to just one song, then we can successfully listen to that song alone.

The contrast mind masquerades by trying to seek the experience of the Source in the body sensations, thoughts and feelings. It conceptualizes and imagines the Sense of Presence in terms of visuals, sounds, and sensations. This is a major hurdle in being in stillness.

Many seekers assume that the Source can be experienced only in the absence of body sensations. They equate the body-less state with the Sense of Presence. Loss of body sensations has nothing to do with the experience of the Source. We can rest in the Sense of Presence despite painful or pleasurable sensations in the body.

Checking

When we practice meditations to access the Source, the contrast mind can masquerade as a checker and attempt to judge the experience. The contrast mind assesses, "Let me see who is experiencing this. Is this experience the same as the actual experience of the Source? Nothing special is happening. After sitting for so long, why am I not becoming thoughtless?"

The mind tries to divert our focus from the experience of the Source by checking, comparing, and judging. If we get entangled in this, we lose our attention on the Source and instead become entrapped by the checking contrast mind. Such checking is the biggest obstacle in abiding in the experience of the Source.

Whenever the contrast mind intervenes and tries to check on the experience, know that it is a trap. The presence of the contrast mind veils the presence of the Source.

The mind, which judges and questions the experience, cannot exist without the living presence of the Source. The very fact that the contrast mind is raising doubts and judgments is only indicating the presence of the Source. Whenever a checker thought arises, simply smile and observe it. Know that the mind is playing a trick. Understand that we don't have to question our awareness; we only need to be present in awareness.

Taking credit for the experience of the Source

With the experience of presence, the contrast mind tries to take credit for having experienced it. An expert pianist is rendering a symphony on the piano. When the performance reaches its peak, the pianist is lost in the performance. He does not exist at that time. All that exists is the performance. However, after the performance, the contrast mind enters and says, "I performed so well!"

By taking credit as being the performer, the contrast mind self-appoints itself to the job of experiencing the Source. The Source can experience itself only when the contrast mind surrenders based on the understanding that the experience of Presence is beyond it.

Whenever the contrast mind tries to take credit, we should realize that it is yet another trick. Tell the mind, "You cannot own the experience. It is only in your absence that the experience of the Source is revealed. Surrender yourself so that the ongoing experience of the Source can be revealed. To the extent that you are still, the experience will shine forth. The more you chatter, the greater the delay in the experience of the Source."

Introspect the Mind – The 'How is My Mind?' Meditation

This meditation technique can be practiced to introspect the functioning of the contrast mind.

Close your eyes and sit in a comfortable posture.

Intermittently ask yourself, "How is my mind?" and watch the thoughts arising within you.

Witness whether your thoughts are rigid, stubborn, or flexible. Your thoughts may have become rigid due to past conditioning. You might not have re-considered them for many years.

See whether the mind is forgiving, giving, grateful, or kind-hearted. Does it feel envious of others' virtues? When does it feel bad or low?

When does the mind work against you and when does it remain your friend?

What does the mind do to get credit? What does it do if it doesn't get credit?

Why does the mind not want to relinquish credit?

In what situations does the mind imitate others?

In what situations does it take a pause for guidance from the Source within?

When is the mind unconscious? When is it aware?

How many of your thoughts are based on past conditioning? What is the basis for the existence of these thoughts?

How can you be free from past conditioning? What habits do you need to inculcate to free yourself?

What is the present state of your mind? What are your repeated thoughts? Why are they repeated so often? What are the thoughts you wish to hold in the future?

Why are you happy at times? Why are you sad at times?

When does the ego feel hurt? When does hatred arise? What is the conditioned thought behind such hatred?

Slowly open your eyes.

When the exploits of the contrast mind are brought to light through introspection, it begins to dissolve. With wisdom, it surrenders and serves as a pure reflective medium for the Source to experience itself.

Part II

Powers of the Source

What is our true nature?

What is at the core of thoughts?

What does it mean to be human?

What is life all about?

The answers to these fundamental questions can be found in the experience of love or peace or bliss. Humans alone are graced with the ability to be aware of these beautiful qualities that express life.

To examine this further, try filling in the blank below. You may just think it up or even write it down:

I would like to lead a life full of_____

Whatever answer you get, ask yourself: what do I wish to experience from such a life? Say, you wrote 'money' as one of the answers. Ask yourself, what do I *really* wish to experience with money? Fill in the blank again now:

I would *really* like to lead a life of _____

Again, what is it that you are really seeking to experience in life when you attempted to answer the second time. If you've written that you would like to lead a life of honesty, ask yourself: what do you wish to gain through honesty? If your answer was health, what do you wish to experience with health? Try it one final time.

I would *really, really* like to lead a life of _____

Most people end up writing qualities such as happiness, courage, abundance, peace, truth, love, fulfillment, harmony, etc. These are the qualities of the Source. They are manifestations of consciousness, expression of our true nature.

In this part of the book, we delve into the essential qualities of the Source and see how our lives can be enriched with these.

Accessing the Source is not just about being in silence. The experience of the Source leads to the expression of the qualities that are described in the pages that follow.

7

The Power of Love
Forgive unconditionally in pure love

Once, a young man was planning to relocate with his family to a new town. He thought of visiting the place to check out its amenities and the neighbourhood so as to assess how safe and comfortable his stay would be.

When he arrived at the town, he struck a conversation with the owner of a small restaurant. "I am considering the merits of moving here with my family. How do you find the people in this town? Do you find them warm and helpful? Can I find a peaceful and loving neighbourhood?"

The old man replied, "How I find the people of this town does not really matter. Tell me… How are the people in the town where you come from?"

"Most of them are nasty and bad-mannered. My neighbours are least loving or caring. They are greedy and quarrelsome. This is why I am checking this place before moving in."

"Bad news… Those are exactly the kind of people you'll find in this town", said the restaurant owner. The man walked away, dejected.

Another passerby visited the same restaurant and asked the owner the same question. The owner asked him, "How are the people in your present neighbourhood?"

"They are sweet God-loving people. We have warm and friendly relations with our neighbours. We always help each other when in need. They have been so affectionate."

"Good news… These are exactly the kind of people you'll find here", said the restaurant owner. The newcomer was happy.

The experience of love and warmth is not dependent on how people behave with us. Our experience of love and warmth hinges on the love that *we* exude, on the warmth that *we* radiate. This is true with any relationship, be it a husband and wife, or parent and child, friends, neighbours, or colleagues.

The word 'Love' has been corrupted through misuse to such an extent that we, as a society, have lost its essential meaning. What is true love?

Just as space permeates everything in the universe, love permeates every part, every aspect of creation. If there is one answer to the question, "How and why does this world exist?" the answer, in one word, is 'Love'. Rather, the answer is 'Pure Love', since the word 'love' has lost its meaning.

Your very existence is an expression of pure unconditional love of the Source (You may call it Consciousness, Creator, God, Divine Self, or any other name). This is the truth of your being.

Pure love is way beyond the personalized love that two or more individuals assert on one another. Pure love has nothing to do with emotions like attachment, attraction, craving, or infatuation that is felt by individuals. Personalized love, though apparently selfless, is rooted in desires and satisfactions.

While unpleasant emotions like anger, hatred or sorrow are considered as negative feelings, people assume attachment (disguised as love) to be a positive virtue. Between two people who are in so-called love, the feelings of jealousy or possessiveness are also misconstrued as love. There cannot be a greater corruption than this.

We have been brought up in a society that judges love based on conditions. Almost all of us have been raised in a belief-system of conditional love. We have been taught that love is something to be earned. We have been made to believe that we can receive love only when we fit into expectations of people. If we are not good enough, we will be deprived of love. If someone does not love us back, they don't deserve our love.

These beliefs have influenced the collective psyche of families, groups, communities, societies since generations to such an extent that love has been reduced to fear of denial. While love is the all-pervasive essence of everything, the false notions of love have caused fear to be perpetuated into all areas of our lives.

It is now time that we, as a society, shift from the paradigm of false conditional love into the essence of pure unconditional love. We need to let go of so many beliefs to be in the essence of pure love.

The Power of Love can be understood based on two powerful principles:

> ***True love can be experienced only through giving,***
> ***not through seeking.***

> ***People who exist in your life are not here to love you.***
> ***They are here to remind you that you are the Source of Love.***

Logical reasoning suggests that we can have something only when we seek it. We live with a mindset that we can experience love only when we acquire it. Howsoever illogical as it may sound, the experience of pure love does not lie in acquiring, but rather in giving it unconditionally. If you receive love, it is merely a bonus.

Love by its nature is giving. It gives boundlessly when it is brimming in life. Everything we see and experience is the expression of love. When you experience true love, you only feel like giving overwhelmingly and unconditionally. It feels great to expect nothing in return!

However, without knowing this, man spends his entire lifetime in seeking love, which often eludes him (or her). He keeps yearning for appreciation, for consideration, for approval from people, due to this fallacy.

For example, someone, who has worked hard all through his work life before retirement and never received any appreciation, breaks down into tears when his office staff speak good things about him at his farewell.

He has waited all those years to hear a few words of praise or approval. Not being aware of the Power of Love has caused him to seek love from the external world.

You can never find true and everlasting love in the external world. Whenever you find yourself feeling deprived of love, you need to remind yourself about this truth.

By knowing that you are the Source of love, you can love yourself, instead of waiting to receive love from the world. Ask yourself: "Why do I need an agent to love myself?" Waiting for the world to love you, is like hiring an agent to love yourself!

It is time for you to honour yourself as the Source of love. You have undertaken this human journey to realize and express the boundless love that you truly are. It is time to embrace love as your true nature.

When you entertain emotions like fear and guilt, you are not honouring your true nature of pure love. You fall out of alignment with the Source. If you truly love yourself, you will never want to hurt yourself through such negative emotions.

When you accept your true nature of love, you move into alignment with the Source. You become one with the Source. This allows love to flow through your human expression.

Deal With the Source, Not the Channels

When man receives anything, he assumes the channel through which he receives to be the Source. As a result, he expects to receive further from the same channel and becomes disheartened if the channel does not deliver the goods.

For example, if his brother, who used to help him earlier, stops helping him, he says, "My brother has let me down." If his father does not assign a share of his property to the son, then the son starts hating his father. This is so because people assume their relatives to be the givers, the Source.

We ignorantly court sorrow when we get habituated to desire from the channels around us. When we need water, we draw it from the tap. Does the tap have any capacity of giving? The tap is merely a channel for the water reservoir. There are many taps (channels) through which water is received, but they all come from the same water reservoir in the building. When we insist that we want water only from a particular tap, we invite sorrow in our lives.

If you seek water directly from the reservoir, you will get more than you could ever ask for. You give up your limited perspective of expecting from a particular channel. As a result, you realize that there are many other channels through which the Source can give. Everything is in abundance in the Source. It is common sense to expect from the Source, rather than the channels.

When you learn to abide in the Source, then your dealings in daily life is with the Source alone. You stop dealing with individuals and begin to see the Source in them. You honour the Source who functions through them. You give to the Source and receive from the Source through all your dealings in the world.

You will not expect anything from individuals as you rest in faith that everything that has to come, will come from the Source.

Loving every aspect of the world

Pure love makes it possible for you to unconditionally love yourself first, so that you have the strength to shower love on others. In fact, when you express love by being the Source, you naturally love the Source *in* others.

Every aspect of the world is an expression of God's will. Out of ignorance, we love a part of this world and refuse to accept the other. Out of fear, we do not embrace the world in its wholeness. By judging or hating the world for its imperfections, we create more of what we judge or hate. All the imperfections that we perceive are actually a shadow cast by our refusal to lovingly accept whatever is.

Pure love is always from the Source for the Source. It is not based on external conditions. It is an illusion if people appear good due to attachment or at fault due to aversion. In reality, from the standpoint of the Source, everyone is faultless, everything exists in perfection. When you see faults in them, you cannot love them. Pure love is experienced when you see the world as a beautiful and faultless expression of the creator.

Pure love is rooted in oneness. It knows no distinction or duality. However, when we assume the limited body-mind as 'I', then it gives birth to the illusory notion of 'others'. This naturally gives rise to delusion, resulting in emotions like anger, fear, greed, hatred, envy, ill-will or resentment.

When we entertain such negative emotions, we succumb to the illusion of separation. In doing so, we actually resist the flow of life through our bodies. It is important to understand that we are indulging in self-sabotage. It is only when we realize this truth that we become prepared to give up all blame, resentment, guilt, and anger against anyone or anything, including ourselves.

There is nothing in this world that can negatively impact us, except our own beliefs, our own thoughts and emotions. Life naturally brings us the experience of love, bliss, peace, health, harmony, vitality and abundance.

Negative, hurtful memories, bitterness, and ill-will choke the free flow of life within us. When one holds onto grudges in life, one feels bitterness and resentment. This clogs the free flow of vital energy. If we feel bitter and hold grudges, in time, it eventually affects our physical wellbeing, causing chronic ailments.

Holding onto negative emotions causes blocks in energy pathways within the mind-body mechanism. These blocks manifest as physiological malfunctions, leading to disease conditions, which eventually erupt as visible symptoms. Chronic headaches, ulcers, indigestion, kidney failures, cancer, are all caused by sustained intensification of negative emotions over long periods of time.

When we resist the free flow of life, it causes us to experience testing circumstances, limitations and sorrow. Actually, these limitations and sorrow come as wake-up calls to re-connect and re-align ourselves with the natural flow of the Source.

By feeling resentment towards any person or situation, we actually plant seeds of hatred. We unknowingly place an order for even more resentment that rebounds back on us, multiplied many times over. We do this unknowingly due to lack of awareness.

With every act in our past where we have either felt hurt or caused others to feel hurt, we have created a string of bondage that blocks free flow in our lives.

How do we get rid of all these strings of bondage, the grudges and bitterness that we have held onto? How do we nullify the seeds of resentment that we have already planted in the past?

By choosing to unconditionally love all those for whom you harbor negative feelings. By forgiving and seeking to be forgiven. Trust this!

Forgiveness helps in removing blocks and harmonizing with nature. It can help in cutting these strings of bondage.

The only way to remove these blockages is by willingly releasing the person or situation with gratitude for what they brought you. We should clearly address all such people –mentally, if not face-to-face– and seek forgiveness for having hurt them. If we have felt hurt, then we need to clearly state that we are now free from the bondage with them by having forgiven them.

The Daily Forgiveness Prayer

Here's a practical exercise that you can perform every night. Before going to sleep, go through your dealings with people during the day without judgment. Wholeheartedly with complete purity of mind, perform the following prayer:

I forgive all those who have hurt me knowingly or
unknowingly today.

I release them from all bondage created due to my feeling hurt.

I sincerely seek forgiveness from all those whom I may have hurt…

…through my thoughts, feelings, words, or actions today.

Please forgive me for not recognizing and honouring the Source within them during my interactions.

Please forgive me; I will try my best not to repeat this in the future.

By doing this, I am not doing a favour on anyone.

I am raising my purity of mind and elevating consciousness.

Thank You for giving me the opportunity to learn and progress.

More than the words, it is the feelings imbued in this prayer that cleanse and release the blocks that clog the free-flow of life.

In this way, you can cut the strings of bondage that bind you to people, and thereby clear the blockages of free flow in your life.

If you have truly and sincerely sought forgiveness or have forgiven someone, you will almost immediately experience an unknown freedom when the invisible bonds have snapped.

You reach a space where you begin to feel grateful to them for having provided you an opportunity to learn and grow.

Forgiveness is incomplete till such time that you haven't forgiven yourself. To be loving and grateful to everything and everyone, first be loving and grateful to yourself. You can never truly love and forgive others unless you love and forgive yourself.

You do this by seeking forgiveness from your own body-mind for any neglect and lack of care in the past. By doing so, you rid yourself of the feeling of guilt and remorse that you have held onto from the past.

By forgiving or seeking forgiveness, you are not doing a favour on anyone. You are ensuring that you reduce your own inner burden of accumulated bondage, which prevents you from flowing with life. The more you practice seeking forgiveness, you find that you begin to feel lighter. Abiding in the Source and creating from the Source becomes easier.

8

Power of Happiness

Let the light that chases after shadows know itself

There was a wise monk, who moved around begging alms with a golden begging bowl gifted to him by the King, who was his disciple.

One night he was about to lie down to sleep in a temple courtyard when he noticed a thief hiding in the dark.

"Here, take this," said the monk, holding out the begging bowl. "See if you can find your happiness with this."

The thief eagerly grabbed the bowl and took off. But he worried sleeplessly through the night, just to make sure that he doesn't get robbed off the golden bowl.

He returned to the monk at daybreak with the bowl. He folded his hands and bowed before the monk, "O venerable one! When you gave away this bowl so freely and happily last night, I felt very poor. I can see that you have slept peacefully without it, while I have lost my sleep to preserve the bowl. What is that wealth within you which made it possible to part with the bowl so easily? I want to acquire that wealth of true happiness."

We know from experience that our basic desire for pure unobstructed happiness is never completely satisfied despite all our efforts to obtain happiness from external objects and situations. Nothing, no one can ever make us perfectly happy. The happiness that we derive from the world is short-lived, and hence we continue to seek more happiness restlessly.

When it is said that we just need to abide in the Source to allow our highest potential to unfold, the obvious question that arises is "What will happen to all those wishes that we have held close to our hearts? We do have unfulfilled desires. Will abiding in the Source guarantee their fulfillment?"

They can be fulfilled. But (be prepared for this) they won't give us true and lasting happiness!

Now, is this bad news? Does this mean that seeking happiness is like chasing after the horizon?

Not at all! On the contrary, when we abide in the experience of the Source, we *are* happiness! Rather, we experience life as the source of causeless happiness.

Imagine someone who has been desperately looking forward to a salary rise. He awaits the letter of rise in his paycheck. Before he receives the letter of salary increment, he discovers that by some way of unexpected inheritance, he has been named the successor to the company where is employed! In that instant of jubilation, he opens his salary increment letter. Now, will the salary hike give him any joy!? He does not need it to be happy anymore!

The unbounded happiness that is experienced in being the Source is like eternal sunlight; all other objects of pleasure or joy dim in comparison as mere candle-flames! So even if our wish-lists were to attain completion, the joy that we imagined in them will be like shadows cast in the blissful light of the Source.

Every effort that we make is driven only by our desire for happiness. Due to our mistaken belief that happiness comes from external objects and situations, we ceaselessly direct our attention and efforts towards the external world.

Desires are incessant streams of thoughts that seek fulfillment from worldly objects or situations. Whenever we acquire the experience of whatever we desire, the restlessness of the mind caused by that desire subsides temporarily. This allows us to experience the happiness that always exists within us, but for a short while.

However, we fail to recognize that the happiness that we thus experience is already present within us. Hence, we wrongly connect the happiness that was experienced with the objects of our desire. The more we experience such momentary happiness, the more convinced we are that we can obtain happiness from people, objects and circumstances outside ourselves. Hence, we continue to desire those things that we believe to be the sources of our happiness. This, at the cost of losing the very source of happiness that is always available within us!

Since the experience of happiness is momentary, we entertain some other desire as soon as the earlier one is fulfilled. We do not realize that this momentary happiness was because we were calm and centered in the stillness of the Source behind thoughts.

The missing link here is that desire, in itself, is never the cause of sorrow, or the lack of happiness. It is the habit of chasing after our desires, borne out of the conviction that happiness lies in their fulfillment that causes sorrow. The habit of desiring veils the ever-present bliss of the Source.

Freedom From Desires – The 'Happy Thoughts' Meditation

We will now practice 'Happy Thoughts' meditation. A 'Happy Thought', in this context, implies an intention to be rid of all desires. As we have seen earlier, the habit of functioning by desires veils the experience of true and permanent happiness. Desires arise in the human mind every moment.

During this meditation, you will maintain the same body posture from the beginning to the end of the meditation session. If you are seated, then you will remain seated till the end. If you are standing, you will remain standing till the end of the meditation session. If you are walking, you will continue to walk.

> In this practice, observe what desires are arising within you. Watch them and tell yourself, "Now, I am free from all desires." Even if you are practicing the meditation for ten minutes, tell yourself, "Now, I am free from all desires at least for the next ten minutes."

Do you know how many desires are there within you? There are several desires which you are not aware of. This meditation helps to bring those desires to light.

As you witness these desires during this meditation, you can get rid of the sorrow caused by these desires.

While practicing the meditation, be cautious about every desire arising within you. Be cautious... Be aware... Witness...

A subtle desire may arise, "It is very hot. Let me stand in the shade." Tell yourself, "I am free from all desires now." Continue your meditation.

Another desire may arise, "My legs are paining. Let me sit for some time." Witness this desire and tell yourself, "I am free from all desires." Continue your meditation.

Whenever any desire arises, just witness it, affirm to yourself that you are free from all desires and continue with the practice.

In this way, remain free from desires during the entire period of this meditation. Don't entertain any desire during this period.

You will be able to easily observe the superficial and predominant desires arising within you. These desires are easily noticeable. However there are certain subtle desires which you cannot easily grasp. Subtler desires are those, wherein we desire that something should *not* happen.

For example, when you want to reach your destination on time, there is a subtle desire that your vehicle should not stop midway. You may not be aware of this desire. You come to know about it only when the vehicle suddenly breaks down or comes to a halt for some reason.

The hindrance in the fulfillment of your desire causes you to experience sorrow. When you observe the rising and falling of desires, both gross and subtle, you begin to realize how desires arise at the first place. You realize the temporary nature of these desires. When they are witnessed for some time without indulging, they subside.

Practicing this meditation is the best way to increase the power of your intention and experience the bliss derived through freedom from desires. Pure happiness that springs from the Source becomes self-evident.

Try to experience this state of freedom at least for 10 minutes.

If you are able to taste the experience of freedom from desires even for a few minutes, the thirst to be rid of all desires can be kindled. Even a glimpse of pure untainted happiness is auspicious, as it instills the perseverance to transcend the realm of thoughts and rest in the blissful presence of the Source.

Our sense of presence is the causeless cause of bliss. Happiness is inherent in the experience that we exist, that we are alive, that we are awake and aware. Just 'being' is enough to experience happiness.

When we try to reason and conceptualize happiness, we indulge in thinking. This takes us far away from the presence of the Source. We seek imaginary happiness in the content of our thoughts.

Seeking happiness in the world is like chasing one's own shadow endlessly. Like the shadow, happiness always eludes us. We experience sorrow, conflict and dissatisfaction when we move away from the Source.

The mind wants to weigh and assess everything on its own terms. The mind thinks, 'Let me first assess and understand this… let me first acquire something… first let me solve my problems… let me confirm that what is being said is the truth; only then will I change my way of life.'

Due to this habit of the mind, it postpones happiness by attaching preconditions to it and keeps waiting to be happy.

Happiness can only be experienced in the present. I AM. LIFE IS. And this, in itself, is the cause for celebration. Life is a celebration! However, this light of bliss is lost in the constant stream of thoughts. We chase after shadows by pursuing our notions about happiness. As a result, we tend to postpone happiness to a time in the future. Happiness can only be experienced here and now, not in the future.

Hence, we need not wait for the fulfillment of any preconditions. We can be happy right here, right now!

True Happiness Beyond the Mind

Whenever you feel dissatisfied or unfulfilled, whenever you sense that you are not 'happy', be sure that the mind is postponing an imagined happiness based on fulfillment of some preconditions. Happiness can never be experienced even if the conditions were to be fulfilled. Instead, the mind will become even more obstinate as its belief in external pursuits is strengthened.

The happiness that the mind seeks can never be experienced. Happiness does not lie in thoughts, or the content of thoughts. True happiness can only be experienced in the state of stillness beyond the mind. There can never be 'peace of mind', since the mind itself is noise. True peace and happiness is always available beyond the mind.

Dissolve Problems With Happiness

We need to look at problems through the perspective of happiness. There is power in happiness. Hence, it is imperative that we remain happy at least during those times when we are in sorrow. This is because no problem can be solved by being in an unhappy state, by fretting or brooding over it.

When viewed from the blissful presence of the Source, problems cease to be 'problems'. We realize that problems don't actually exist. They are situations that serve as opportunities for expressing the qualities of the Source – qualities like creativity, love, happiness, courage, compassion, and patience.

We have believed that achieving desirable results alone can lead to happiness. The truth is exactly the opposite. Being in the state of happiness attracts desirable results.

When witnessed from the blissful standpoint of the Source, problems need not be solved; they dissolve! You actually witness the problem move towards resolution by being in the experience of the Source.

The World Needs Happy Thinkers

When people become prepared to function consciously for manifesting divine qualities on Earth, many possibilities get expressed through them. Clarity manifests within them in the form of foresight and truth-discernment. They remain happy every moment regardless of the circumstances around them. Such people serve the world in a big way by leading an impersonal altruistic life. More than their actions, their happy presence serves as an invisible magnet to attract higher possibilities into the world.

Being the presence of the Source causes the light of pure happiness to shine forth. This light of pure happiness radiates all around us and touches the lives of people. It awakens the Source within those around us.

We can invoke the power of happiness by looking at people with the eye of happiness; by connecting with people from the presence that we truly are. Happiness is infectious. It has a resonating effect on the people around us. Happiness is a powerful creative force that brings about positive transformation in the world. Hence, abiding in the natural happy state of the Source is the greatest service.

9

Power of Peace

Welcome the Source to work in life

In the dead of night, a young man sat beside a river, waiting for the light of dawn so that he could cross.

As he waited, his foot touched a bag of stones. The man picked up the bag and, to pass time, he removed a stone and threw it into the river. He felt good listening to the sound it made.

He saw a dog running by the shrubs. He picked up another stone from the bag and threw it at the dog. He then remembered a recent incident in which his friend had abused him. To vent his frustration, he threw yet another stone into the river.

In this way, he continued throwing the stones - one after another. At sunrise, he looked into the bag and saw that one last stone was left... a beautiful, large and precious diamond!

He couldn't believe that he had thrown away so many beautiful diamonds – all because he was bored, frustrated and not paying attention.

True and lasting peace, like the diamonds that the young man was squandering away, is already available within us. Without this knowledge, people indulge at lower levels of consciousness.

Very often individuals seek happiness through measures that are stimulating to a lower level of consciousness. These come in the form of greed, lust, and conflict, to name just a few.

They have yet to experience the higher levels of bliss that exist in the experience of the Source. They have yet to realize that not only are these higher levels already available to them, but will actually bring about a more lasting and fulfilling peace.

The Creator's Perspective

Imagine a painter who paints the picture of a paintbrush. This picture of the paintbrush comes alive and serves to create more paintings for the painter.

However, if the paintbrush assumes its own individual existence and a separate personal purpose, it would go about painting without consulting the painter. Though it was created to explore and manifest the painter's creative inspiration, the paintbrush will do everything else without seeking to fulfill the painter's wish.

In the same way, the human body-mind mechanism is the Creator's creation, which serves as an instrument or medium to manifest the Creator's further creations. However, human beings perceive and operate individualistically instead of allowing the Creator to experience and express through them.

Though a lot of individual and group creations may be happening in the visible realm, yet they are devoid of true and lasting contentment, since the Creator's purpose remains unfulfilled.

Consider a sheet of paper on which letters are written. Each written letter contributes to the overall story that the author wishes to express. However, if any single letter were to decide to express itself differently, will the story flow as the author intended?

If a single letter were to look around the sheet and compare itself with the other letters, it may find some letters that are bigger in size, some that are in italics, some are bolded and hence standout. This letter may then feel dejected by comparing thus and wish that it should be like the others, or perhaps even better. However, unless the letter attains the perspective of the author or surrenders to his will, the very purpose of why it was penned on the paper is lost.

If we draw a parallel to human life, we see that individual human life is an expression on the stage of life, contributing to the overall plan of the creator. If any person gets into the game of comparison and the need for superiority and enacts such tendencies, it becomes an abnormality, a deviation to the grand plan of the creator.

We can manifest the Creator's plan only when the first creation happens first. The first creation is the act of seeking inspiration from the creator within by accessing the inner peace that exists in the background of our mind.

You need to allow Peace to work in your life. When you surrender your life situations to the Source, life progresses naturally and smoothly towards its highest potential.

Peace is a natural trait of who you truly are. Sadly, more people have adopted sorrow, distress and conflict as regular habits and have become blind to any other path. Many of them don't realize that these choices are perhaps only making it more difficult for them to experience peace.

They are undoubtedly equally unaware of the consequences of living like this. When an individual experiences unhappiness, instead of searching for a path to permanent peace, he tends to complain more. This only further shrouds his happy natural state. That's why when you're unhappy, place inner peace at the top of your priority list. As a matter of truth, inner peace should come much before your priority list!

When you truly understand the Source and its nature through experience, you intuitively understand the importance of peace. One of the primary reasons to uphold peace is because it is the essence of existence, an aspect of the Presence that operates through your mind and body.

It's your natural state which is accessible to you at any time. It's veiled due to lack of awareness. *When you become aware, you'll realize that you need not* be *peaceful – you* are *peace.* It is your essential nature, and the more you operate from this natural state, the greater your sensitivity and understanding. Your clarity and awareness about everything that's happening within and around you will also increase. By consistently reminding yourself to be in peace, you attain supreme consciousness.

Unhappiness and sorrow are habits. But they don't become habits overnight. No one wakes up one morning and says "I'm unhappy and I'll stay this way for the rest of my life." Unhappiness is a condition that has been imposed on us from childhood. Toddlers' natural method of learning is through observation of their surroundings and imitating what they see. If they see adults around them being unhappy, discontented and complaining, then that is what they'll learn and adopt.

We need to be realistic with our expectations of happiness. We all pass through periods of unhappiness on occasion. So what should we do when we discover we've become unhappy? The answer is simple – put peace first. Putting peace first means developing a habit of placing serenity and happiness above all else. The moment we become unhappy, we need to remind ourselves to return to happiness and invoke the Peace of the Source.

One of the best ways to hone this ability is by living in a higher state of awareness. You need to become aware of what's happening to your level of happiness after you witness an incident – any incident. You need to pay attention to your state of happiness after you interact with someone, or after someone praises or criticizes you; or someone behaves in a particular way towards you. It could be that your level of happiness changes even when someone gives you a piece of his mind.

Through all of these situations, if you find you're losing awareness and your level of consciousness drops, you haven't put peace first. If your level of consciousness rises and you still feel joyful, then you have succeeded at putting peace first.

Many incidents affect your level of consciousness. By appearance, they seem to be caused by the actions of others. In reality the incidents have nothing to do with lowering of your consciousness. You have allowed your level of consciousness to be lowered. In effect, you've let go of peace – you've surrendered your peace to something else.

Your level of consciousness can remain low even for hours after incidents. You can, no doubt, recall incidents from your past. At the time they had occurred, had you known your consciousness was being stolen, you'd have been more careful. At that time, had you observed, "I'm allowing my peace to be shrouded by clouds of irritation," you wouldn't have let go of peace – you never would have surrendered it to the situation.

Never surrender your peace in any situation; instead, surrender the situation to peace. Give peace a chance to work in your life.

Only when you're at peace do you experience true happiness. True happiness arises from within. It's not dependent on any external cause. Happiness should never be confused with the exhilaration or excitement you experience after a party or a movie. True happiness is the calm bliss you experience when you meditate, when you're flowing with creativity and spontaneity, when you're at peace with yourself, when you feel one with everything.

From this state of peaceful being, you'll naturally rise towards love, creativity, harmony, abundance and vitality effortlessly. It's what can be called an effortless effort. When you're at peace with yourself, neither internal nor external situations will be able to shake you.

Good Morning Peace

When you are sitting in meditation, you are not doing 'nothing'. Your presence is doing a lot. Practice peace meditation with this understanding. If you practice peace meditation in the right way, then your presence can usher World peace.

It is important to understand that an individual can never bring peace, because individuality is noise in itself. With this peace meditation, peace alone can bring peace.

> Whenever there is a negative emotion, close your eyes and calmly repeat to yourself the phrase "Good Morning Peace!" Whatever thought appears, say, "Good Morning Peace" after that thought. Greet every thought with these three words.

> The idea is to interrupt the train of unwanted thoughts that continue unabated, using the words "Good Morning Peace!" as a mantra. When you utter these words to every thought and wait for the next thought and say it again, your thoughts disappear after some time eventually leading you into a thoughtless state.

When you chant this phrase, the words inspire and empower you to feel peace and to help it take hold in your heart.

Consider you are at work and a strongly worded e-mail arrives from a colleague questioning one of your actions. Your first response may be to send a strongly worded e-mail response yourself. Instead, close your eyes and greet every thought that arises with the words, "Good Morning Peace!"

After a few minutes, open your eyes and see what reply emerges from the Source. Create a space where the most unexpected solutions can arise from the peaceful presence of the Source.

Learn to see problems being solved by accessing peace. When you say "Good Morning Peace," you invite Peace to take over. This will guarantee inner peace and powerfully propel you to create the future you want.

When you practice this meditation in your daily situations, you are actually invoking Peace to work in your life. You are surrendering the situation to Peace. Allow Peace take care of the situation.

Close your eyes and witness your thoughts.

Thoughts that occur within you are just noise. When this noise stops, then peace gets an opportunity to reveal itself. Peace has not gone anywhere. It should only get an opportunity to work.

If any individual wishes to bring peace, he cannot. But by surrendering himself, he gives the opportunity for peace to bring peace.

So right now, how should your presence be, for peace to manifest? The individual need not worry about how peace will work.

What happens when a little child is playing with its toys? Some of his toys are broken and scattered. When the child goes to sleep, his mother comes and neatly puts everything back in order.

How did the child help the situation? The child helped by keeping quiet and sleeping. It allowed the mother to come in and restore order.

In the same way, take a look at the issues that surround you in life. There may be problems related to relationships or health, money or neighbourhood. The highest way to solve all these scattered problems is to rest in the inner stillness of the Source and allow Peace to bring Peace. Allow Peace to bring solutions.

After welcoming Peace by saying "Good Morning Peace!" you can open your eyes with the understanding that Peace will now look at the world through these eyes.

With this practice, you return to the inner silence and allow Peace to work. You become a medium for raising mass consciousness.

10

Power of Presence
Shift to Pure Awareness

A wise old man was relaxing on the deck of a cruise ship and reading a book. His face had a serene glow. He had become the topic of discussion among the passengers who walked past him. They all began to consider him a spiritual master of some sort.

Suddenly the captain announced a storm and requested all passengers to return to their rooms. Everyone ran from the deck into their rooms. It was almost an hour by the time the storm had passed.

The captain of the ship walked past the deck to inspect the mast. He was surprised to see the old man still there. His book was drenched and so he had kept it aside and was calmly watching the sea.

The captain went up to him and asked him, "Sir, were you here all the while? Weren't you afraid of the waves that were flooding the deck?"

The old man smiled, "Oh! I was indeed afraid. I too ran and took shelter. While the others may have rushed into their rooms, I remained still and took shelter within myself!"

A clear glimpse of our true nature can awaken us from our limiting beliefs and shift us onto the enlivening presence that we truly are.

Presence is the wakeful awareness of life itself. Presence or 'being' is the basis of existence. Presence comes first; thinking comes later. To think, you have to first be. Presence is your true nature. It is the awareness of your existence.

Presence is the most obvious truth about you. Yet, it is lost in the constant chatter of thoughts. Thinking cannot lead to the experience of presence. To experience presence, you need to be aware of what *is*… right here, right now.

A Greek philosopher had once stated, "I think, therefore I am". However, if existence were dependent on thinking, then we would not exist if we were to stop thinking. This is certainly not the case. When we are in deep sleep, we do not think. And yet, we do exist. We even comment on waking that we had a sound sleep. We have to exist during deep sleep to be able to know that we did sleep well.

Presence is independent of thought. Presence just *is*.

Our sense of presence is the simple truth that we are constantly and spontaneously aware of. It is because we are present that we engage in all kinds of activities. "I am reading this book." "I am" comes first. It is because "I am" that "I am reading." And "I am aware that I am reading."

We tend to be lost in whatever follows 'I am…' I am a man, I am reading, I am smart, I am sad, I am an artist. Everything that follows 'I am' is subject to change. But the 'I am' is constant. It is the constant sense of presence that enlivens all activities of life.

Presence is the most obvious experience. It is the open secret – so open and obvious that we easily fail to notice it.

> Suppose a soft sound is constantly playing in the background during the day while you are engaged in your daily activities, you will soon get habituated to it. After a few hours, you will lose awareness of this sound, even though it continues to play. It is only when the sound stops momentarily that you become aware of its existence.

Similarly, the sense of presence is ceaselessly going on ever since our body was born. We may change our identity – from being a child to becoming an adolescent, from being a youth to a middle-aged family maker, from being a student to one who earns a living, from being a parent to being a grandparent. However, the sense of presence remains unchanged; it remains constant. If you were to take away all the roles that define you, you would still exist!

All the affairs of the world happen in the presence of the sun. Flowers blossom in the presence of the sun. Human life is dependent on the sun. Man wakes up at sunrise and retires after sunset. But the sun does not wake anyone up, nor does it put anyone to sleep. It is merely present. All activities still happen owing to the presence of the sun. Similarly, everything – including thinking – happens in the presence of who you truly are.

Unconditional happiness is experienced when Presence becomes aware of itself, when "I am aware that I am", when consciousness becomes conscious of itself. This happiness is pure, independent of external factors. In fact it is the source of happiness. When you are aware of this constant living presence, you are being aware of your pure undeniable existence. It is being awake to the light that shines upon everything that is being known.

Thoughts – whether they are trivial and mundane, or brilliant and revolutionary – serve merely as a medium to indicate the presence of the Source. This is the whole and sole purpose of thoughts.

Experiencing the Presence, the Source, through the medium of thoughts can also be understood as the second news. We always focus on the first news that the content of our thoughts convey.

Suppose that a thought occurs: "It's such a lovely, bright and sunny day!" While this is the content of the thought, it is actually also conveying the news that *you are alive*. In other words, the second news is: *"I am"* or *"Consciousness exists"*. We usually get caught up with the first news and so the second essential news is lost.

As a daily practice, you can raise your awareness of the second news. You are flooded with various bits of information every minute. With every such input, you can remember the second news.

Having read this, a thought might arise in your mind, "How can I ignore important news and just live with the truth that Consciousness exists?"

No. This does not mean that you should ignore the happenings of the world. Of course, you will heed them and take necessary action. However, everything that happens is an opportunity, an invitation, to shift to the underlying truth —that the Source is enlivening all this.

In this way, shift your attention from the body-mind to Consciousness. Turn back your attention from the objects of perception to that which enables perception, from thought to that which enables thinking. You will then rise above the changing and limited to that which is changeless, eternal and boundless.

There is nothing to be *done* to experience Presence. Thoughts may continue to occur, actions may be taken, however they need not interfere with the awareness of Presence. Presence is experienced beyond doing and non-doing.

When you abide in awareness of Presence, you go beyond the body. Bodily sensations may continue to be felt, actions may happen, but there will be a constant awareness of this formless Presence, of just being alive. The more you practice being aware of Presence, the more it will become obvious in your everyday activities.

When you operate from this formless presence, by not assuming yourself as a body but knowing yourself as the conscious presence, events in your life will automatically steer their course towards the ultimate goal of life. This is the beauty of presence.

Acquire the art of simply *being* in pure formless presence. People who perform their labors in this manner bring presence to their thoughts, feelings, words and actions. Creation then happens from the Source effortlessly.

Accessing the Presence behind thoughts – the *'I am'* meditation

You can learn how to be aware of presence through the practice of 'I am' meditation. This meditation is the art of simply resting in pure presence. It brings forth the experience of pure consciousness.

Before beginning your meditation, set a timer. Be seated in a comfortable meditative posture and close your eyes. You need not necessarily follow the yogic meditative posture that has become commonplace. It's important to be comfortable so that your physical body does not pull your attention.

This meditation will be practiced using *"I am"* as an anchor. Read the directions a few times until you fully understand and are comfortable using them. Or if you wish, you may record the following instructions and listen to them during the meditation.

> Keep your body still and listen to the sounds around you. Identify at least five different sounds. Don't rush through this. With a quiet mind, focus your attention on each sound without paying special attention to any single one. Identify each sound and then move on to the next.
>
> With each sound, there are other subtle sounds. Listen to them attentively: conversations of people, clattering dishes, children playing, the running engines of vehicles, objects falling. Depending on where you are seated, you may also hear other sounds like footsteps, television, music, chirping of birds, dogs barking,

water flowing, whistling, someone laughing, or crying. These are examples of ordinary sounds around us.

As you're listening to the various sounds, notice the presence of your own awareness in which these sounds are arising. For this noticing to take place, ask yourself, "Who is listening to these sounds?" The answer will arise within you: "I am". Repeat the words 'I am' a few times and dwell in the feeling of 'I am'. This phrase anchors you to the space where the presence of the one who knows the sounds is being sensed.

Next, watch your breath. Feel the air passing through your nostrils as you inhale and exhale. Try to identify whether the air is warm or cold when you inhale and exhale. If your attention strays, bring it back to your breath. See whether the breath went in silently or with a sound, and whether it came out silently or with a sound, whether the breath was shallow, deep, or heavy. However your breath is, know it without attaching any labels or trying to regulate it.

As you notice your breath, notice the presence of your own consciousness in which breath is arising. To do this, after a few moments of observing your breath, ask yourself, "Who is noticing the breath?" Repeat the phrase a few times, 'I am' as an anchor to place you in the space where the presence of the one who knows the breath is being sensed.

Now turn your attention to your body. If there is stiffness or pain in any part of your body, identify the pain. Be aware of the various sensations in your body. Which areas feel light or heavy? Which parts of your body touch your clothes? Which areas itch, are dry, or sweat? Continue until you've felt everything.

While you are noticing your body sensations, also notice the one who is knowing these sensations. Now shift to the one who is knowing by repeating the words 'I am' as an anchor. Be in the sense of presence in which these sensations are being felt.

Next, shift your attention to thoughts arising within. After identifying a thought, let it go. There is no need to pursue it. Now identify the next thought.

After watching your thoughts for some time, ask yourself, "Who is knowing these thoughts?" The answer will arise, "I am." Know the knower. Without moving the body, know the knower of these thoughts. Repeat the words 'I am' as an anchor and continue being in this state. Rest in this feeling of presence that witnesses thoughts.

After being in this state for few minutes, open your eyes. While continuing with your activity, dwell in the experience of 'I am'. Contemplate on the understanding you've gained from the experience.

Whenever you practice this meditation, remember to first watch each aspect: listening, breathing, sensations, and thoughts. With each, experience the presence that is observing these aspects.

You may even catch the mind trying to imagine Presence by knowing it in terms of thoughts, words, or mental images. However, your existence is beyond all of this. The mind cannot see it. When the mind is unable to see something, it begins to try and imagine it. Instead of imagining, just experience your presence; rest in the feeling of being alive and awake.

By practicing this meditation every day, you can experience freedom from the clutter of thoughts and open to the bliss that is experienced in being the Source. Even if you do not practice it every day, raise your awareness whenever possible to the truth of the constant presence that you essentially are. The knowing and witnessing is always ongoing.

11

Power of Acceptance
Dissolve resistance to life situations

An elderly woman and her little grandson, whose face was sprinkled with bright freckles, spent the day at the zoo. Many children were waiting in a queue to get their cheeks painted by a local artist who was decorating them with tiger paws.

"You've got so many freckles, there's no place to paint!" a girl in the line said to the little boy. Embarrassed, the little boy dropped his head.

His grandmother knelt down next to him. "I love your freckles. When I was a little girl I always wanted freckles," she said, while tracing her finger across the child's cheek. "Freckles are beautiful!"

The boy looked up, "Really?"

"Of course," said the grandmother. "Why, just name me one thing that's prettier than freckles." The little boy thought for a moment, peered intensely into his grandma's face and softly whispered, "Wrinkles!"

If the lily were to be jealous of the rose, it won't be able to appreciate its own beauty and uniqueness.

When we resist any part of our lives, it causes sorrow. Accepting the way nature has shaped our lives makes it possible for us to appreciate ourselves and celebrate our uniqueness.

Man lives with the illusion that he can prevent any situation from affecting him by resisting it. On the contrary, he is only increasing his woes by resisting his life situations.

When you resist any situation, you give attention to it. The situation worsens as you energize it through your resistance. What you resist persists.

If we visualize sorrow as a river, then the source of this river is resistance. The moment we resist something, it gives birth to the river of sorrow.

If we continue to resist the given life situation, it is like building banks on either side of this river of sorrow. The banks of resistance constrict the flow, thereby deepening the river of sorrow.

When these banks of resistance are removed through acceptance, suffering dissolves, just like water that dissipates when it is allowed to flow. Acceptance dissolves sorrow in the infinite expanse of the Source.

When you allow people and situations to be the way they are, you are neither causing nor constricting the flow of the river of sorrow.

Resistance is the source of all sorrow, while acceptance is the key to happiness. Sorrow meets its end in the moment of complete acceptance.

There may be times when your mind is so agitated that it may seem impossible to access the Source. It may seem that the whirlwind of negative emotions may not allow the Source to shine. At such times, accessing the peaceful bliss of the Source seems farfetched, if not impossible. What do you do when gripped by such feelings?

When you are faced with a situation that causes resistance within you, you can fall back to the restful presence of the Source with the help of a simple question. This question is like a magic key that enables you to transcend all feelings and access the ever-present peace.

Accept your thoughts and feelings – "Can I accept this?"

In situations when there is resistance and when you find it difficult to access the Source, ask yourself a simple question, "Can I accept this?" "This" being whatever is happening at this particular moment. Whenever an unfavorable incident occurs, ask yourself, "*Can I accept this?*"

"Can I accept this?" This small mantra can work wonders in your life. Whenever a minor incident occurs, you'll find that the answer will be mostly yes. The moment you say yes, you will notice that negative emotions and all thoughts drop and you dip into the Source automatically, though just for a few moments.

Is this practical? It may not sound workable. Yet, as the popular adage goes, the proof of the pudding is in the eating. We can't realize the magic of acceptance until we have tried it and experienced it for ourselves.

In trivial incidents that you resist, you'll find that this mantra works 99% of the time! For example, if someone insults you, ask yourself, "Can I accept this?" If your answer is yes, you are free at once.

Situations are facts. They are the way they are, whether you agree or not. Resisting facts results in fear, sorrow and frustration. Resistance destroys your ability to solve and tends to worsen the situation.

Your inner resistance to situations does not do any good to handling them effectively. By letting go and accepting the situation you give a chance for peace to resolve it.

The moment you let go, you will find that you are able to see more clearly. You tap into the creative potential of the Source and are able to discover solutions that you could never have seen before.

Through the continued use of this method, many of your problems will be solved. Make a habit of asking, "Can I accept this?" Imagine that something goes wrong as soon as you wake up in the morning. Perhaps you've been woken and disturbed out of sound sleep by barking dogs. You may be annoyed about it. Whatever be the case, just ask, "Can I accept this?" If you're able to accept the noise, then you'll say, "Let it continue. If the dogs are barking, let them bark, I accept it." Acceptance brings an instant feeling of relief.

If the answer to this mantra is, "No, I cannot accept this," then accept your non-acceptance. This is the key. If you feel, "I can't tolerate hearing those dogs barking," then ask, "*Can I accept my non-acceptance?*" If worry is eating you, ask yourself, "Can I accept this worry... just for this moment?" Your answer will likely be, "Alright, so I'm worried. I accept it."

By accepting your non-acceptance, something new is created, and you'll be amazed at the results. In essence, you're saying, "Ok, this is how I am. I have faults, I am seeing flaws with the world around me, but I'm fine with myself. I completely accept myself as I am in this moment." A person who can't accept himself might say, "I have an ugly nose. I can't accept this." But with this mantra he'll say, "Alright, can I now accept this non-acceptance? Of course, I can!"

It's possible that you'll answer negatively in some situations. If that happens, give yourself some time and ask again. If you still feel something isn't acceptable, give yourself even more time and ask again, "Can I accept this now?" You'll see that after some time, a positive answer will emerge. It may not come about immediately, but after a few minutes or perhaps even a few hours, you'll say yes. Once you're able to say yes and accept the situation you'll instantly feel relieved.

When you are resisting a situation, your mind is not open to all the possible options that exist. For the troubled and unclear mind, options seem to be limited. The state of such a mind is like driving the vehicle of life with a hazy windscreen. Common sense demands that you must wipe the windscreen clean so that your journey of life is safe. Accepting the life situation helps clear the windscreen of the vehicle of life.

THE SOURCE • 106

You may wonder whether you can achieve what you want if you keep submitting to everyday situations. Acceptance is not about being submissive or passive to the happenings of the world.

Accepting and Allowing lead you to a space where the mind opens up to all the possible options for a solution - it does not mean you're in denial or running away from your problems.

The problem does not remain as-is when you accept it. The moment you accept the situation, a new way of solving the problem presents itself. The solution is revealed to you intuitively from the Source. The moment you resist a problem, you're actually blocking this marvelous process from working for you.

If you're experiencing a particularly difficult time in accepting a situation or individual, here are four steps to help you overcome your obstacles:

- Wait for some time and try to accept it again.

- Accept only part of the situation. Accept it in steps, one part at a time.

- Accept only the negative feeling that the situation has caused.

- Accept not being able to accept it. This is a very critical step. Ask yourself, "Can I accept that I cannot accept it?"

When you are able to say, "Yes" to "Can I accept this?" you've released any negative feelings associated with it. What a relief that is! You may consider this a small even insignificant step, but it really isn't. Doing even this much causes a major shift in your consciousness. When this shift occurs, your mind automatically begins to accept a number of related and similar issues. You begin to attract more positivity toward you!

In chemistry, a litmus test determines whether a given solution is acidic or not, or whether an intended chemical reaction was successful. Similarly, a simple test can tell you whether your act of acceptance was successful. When you have accepted something, you gain a fresh perception of larger problems or life situations; you begin to see them in a new light.

All you have to do is review the situation in your mind, look at the problem again, and if your acceptance has worked, then it should seem lighter and clearer. If there is still some negative emotion left, then once again ask the question: "Can I accept this?" You'll review the situation in your mind yet again. Has it lightened? Keep doing this until it's completely clear.

Learning the higher lessons of life

Life is a journey of learning. It is when the going is not to our liking that we learn the most in life. Situations that seem difficult are actually opportunities to learn and mature. Accepting your life situations can make you experientially realize that whatever is happening with you right now is what you need for your growth. The understanding, '*This is exactly what I need in this moment of life*' brings your mind into a frame of acceptance.

At this time whatever you are receiving, be it respect, abuse, violence, love, good or bad behavior from people, it is your need of the moment. It has come to teach you vital lessons of life, to help you grow. However repulsive or disagreeable it may seem, as soon as you recognize the current situation as the fulfillment of a higher need, your stress about it will cease.

When seen this way, negative feelings actually serve as reminders for you to breakout and dip into the experience of the Source. The moment you sense a negative feeling, treat it as a higher calling to shift to the presence of consciousness.

If you try to resist or suppress negative feelings, they usually come back later, even stronger. If you explode, then you feel more negative with guilt. You can take action based on your negative feelings, but only after you've accepted and neutralized them. *Any action taken on a platform of negativity is usually counterproductive and it only backfires.*

Acceptance is the springboard on which you can dive into the Source and transcend these feelings. Neutralize negative feelings through acceptance. When you sense a negative feeling like sorrow, anger, fear, helplessness, hopelessness, guilt or resentment, ask yourself the question, *"Can I accept this feeling as it is?"*

Just be with the feeling and allow it to be as it is. Hold it for however long you can, knowing that it will vanish, especially if you don't get involved in the reasons surrounding the feeling. That's not to say another feeling won't surface. If it does, just accept this one and be with that feeling too. Continue in this way until you reach a peaceful state.

Another question that can cause a shift is, "*Is this feeling the problem, or is my non-acceptance of this feeling the real problem?*"

When you ask yourself this question, you will find that in 100% of the cases, the problem is with your non-acceptance of the feeling.

The next question you can ask is "*Will I be happier by being in this feeling, or by releasing this feeling?*"

You will notice that as the feeling is released, you'll be left in a relaxed, thoughtless state of peace. Feelings are closest to the Source. When you dive deep into your feelings by accepting them, you access the Source – you experience peace.

The smallest act of letting go helps you in every facet of your life. Not only are you free mentally, but it positively affects you physically, emotionally, socially, and spiritually. It sets off a chain reaction that reverberates through your entire being, leading you to a state of higher consciousness.

12

Power of Detachment

Rising above the pull of duality

Two monks, who were wandering through the forest, reached the bank of a river. They found a young woman who sat weeping, because she was afraid to cross the river without help. She begged the two monks to help her.

The younger monk turned away. The monks of their order were forbidden from touching a woman. But the older monk picked up the woman without a word and carried her across the river. He set her down on the other side and quietly continued his journey.

The younger monk who followed him tried to be silent during the day, but then couldn't contain himself. Finally, he asked his senior, "Touching a woman is a violation of our principles. You shouldn't have carried her."

The older monk turned to the younger one. "I only carried her across the river. You have been carrying her all day!"

Detachment is an inner state; it is a quality of the Source. Detachment is not a state of mind; rather, it is a state of witnessing the mind without being attached to its beliefs or impressions.

If we notice our inner self-talk, most of us will find that a lot of attention and energy is wasted in holding onto our fixed notions and beliefs – the filters through which we see the world. These mental fixations are like the burden that the younger monk continued to carry on his back.

Most people tend to be victim to the pull of tendencies throughout their lives. We can abide in the Source beyond the duality of the world only when we free ourselves from this cycle.

Where there is life, death always follows. Joy is followed by sorrow. Similarly, praise and insult, success and failure, like and dislike, follow each other and the cycle goes on.

The Power of Detachment rids us from the pull of attachments and aversions. It enables us to transcend the pull of desires and yet, enjoy the world.

Desire by itself isn't the real problem. It is attachment to desire that leads to endless seeking, craving and frustration. Attachment implies a sense of obsession, infatuation or fixation. To be free from attachment is to be free from suffering and to be free from suffering is to embrace bliss.

Attachment to relationships, roles that we play at home and the workplace, titles, money, comforts and conveniences, lead to the tendency of acquisition and preservation. Being identified with the limited individual personality, we are constantly engaged in acquiring what we lack and preserving what we fear we may lose. This tendency of acquisition and preservation is a vicious cycle that is propelled by attachment.

When a person is infatuated with someone, he does not know he has got attached to that person because he does not realize when it happens. Attachment is disguised as love and creates an invisible bondage. It's the same with addictions. Addiction is an attachment to things that cause a pleasurable experience.

> Review your life. Where are you attached? You may think that it is love and not attachment. But you really have to redefine it, whether truly, it is love or attachment. People do not know the true meaning of love and therefore mistake lust and attachment for love. They are entrapped in attachment, all the while believing it to be love.

Anger also stems from attachment. Anger cannot arise without attachment. People assume anger as a negative trait and attachment (disguised as love) to be a positive virtue. However, both are deeply related to each other. They are two sides of the same coin called attachment. Ultimately both lead to suffering and discontentment.

How to Get Over Attachment?

Attachment or obsession occurs when you live as a claimant, claiming ownership of objects, relationships, homes, etc. When you lay aside your claims, knowing that these objects and relationships are impermanent and have no bearing whatsoever on your state of happiness, you will no longer be attached to external objects or people.

Each day remind yourself, "I am a guest in this world, and a guest does not lay claim to the things in the house. I am grateful that I am privileged to make use of the things in the house, but do not become attached to them."

Receive everything that comes to you in the wrapper of detachment. Your prayer will change, "O God! Please let me receive whatever comes in life in the wrapper of detachment."

As long as you are here in this world, make use of the things around you, but do not let them use you. Use your mind, but do not get attached to it. Your mind is an amazing friend if you are not attached to it. However, the mind can work against you if it controls you.

Does this mean that you lose your love and passion for life and its affairs? Not at all! The passion will still be there, and yet, it will be a *detached* passion. The love will be unconditional and unbroken. You will no longer be imprisoned by what you engage with in the world.

For example, your spouse can no longer make you angry or make you happy. Your emotional state is within your control. It doesn't mean you stop loving this person. It means you relinquish them of the responsibility of making you feel a certain way; and you become independent of their power to make you feel a certain way. Your love then flows boundlessly every moment without discrimination, for you love your Self–your very aliveness–within everyone and everything!

Letting Go of the One Who is Attached

World views are actually mind-views. This world of perceptions is not actually happening "out there". It exists in the mind and is made up of your beliefs, prejudices and impressions that bind you to your perception of the world. This is of value only if it is realized through direct experience, not merely at a conceptual or intellectual level.

At a fundamental level, it's about detachment from thoughts. The content of your thoughts shapes your beliefs and your world. Detachment, then, is about giving up the affinity for the content of thoughts. It's about being in a state of indifference to the content of thoughts.

You cannot be free by letting go of your attachment to any particular belief or person, because it is then replaced by something or someone that you consider to be 'better'. In other words, you cannot give up anything, unless you hold onto something that seems 'better'. And then you get attached to the 'better' thing!

True freedom from all attachment happens when you let go of the one who is attached – the limited separate individual who you assume yourself to be.

We tend to forget that as long as we live in the illusion of our limited personality, we have to suffer the poison of attachment. If we cling to our limited separate identities, we are bound to experience fear, sorrow and anger. From attachment springs the fear that our desire may not be fulfilled, sorrow when the desire does not bear fruit, and anger with whosoever or whatever seems to have obstructed it.

Where does the solution lie?

It lies in steering clear from thoughts that are based on the limited 'I', 'me', and 'mine'. Insulate yourself from the grip of the limited personality through the practice of detachment. You need to first rise above them and see them for what they truly are. This can happen only when you learn to watch your thoughts by being centered in the Source.

Categorizing Thoughts – The A-B-C-D Meditation

Let us look at one more way of accessing the Source that helps in breaking attachment to thoughts.

In this meditation, the first four letters of the alphabet, A, B, C and D, are used to watch your thoughts and gradually reach a state beyond thoughts. You categorize thoughts into four types:

A – Affirmative, B – Bad, C – Circumstantial, D – Delusional.

Close your eyes and allow your thoughts to emerge unhampered. Observe the flow of your thoughts.

The moment you get a thought, ask yourself whether it belongs to A, B, C or D category.

Call all positive thoughts that make you feel good as 'A' Thoughts – Affirmative thoughts: "I am beginning my vacation tomorrow", "All my friends are very helpful", "My child makes me proud" are all examples that fall in this category.

'B' or Bad thoughts are ones that do not generate a good feeling in you. These are thoughts such as "My boss always chides me",

"My children speak rudely nowadays", "My spouse always nags me when I get home", "Why do bad things always happen to me?"

"C" thoughts or Circumstantial thoughts are those that relate to the environment or the body. "A breeze is blowing", "It is getting hot", "I am hungry", are all examples of this type of thoughts.

Usually an 'A' thought or a 'B' thought follows. In that case, notice and label both. For example, "I love this breeze" is an 'A' thought which might follow the 'C' thought of noticing the breeze. Similarly, I am irritated that I am hungry is a 'B' thought that follows the 'C' 'thought of noticing your hunger.

'D' thoughts or Delusional thoughts are those that you don't know where to place in 'A', 'B' or 'C'. Thus, anything that confuses you could be labeled a 'D' thought.

For a decided time, continue labeling thoughts as A, B, C, or D.

Before we understand the meditation further, try it for five to ten minutes. As always, a timer helps. This meditation is best done with closed eyes though you could graduate, with some practice, to doing it with open eyes too.

When you practice this meditation, you will eventually experience moments of thoughtlessness. Then another thought arises and again you label a thought and wait for the next thought. Again, you rest in the experience of the Source.

When you break the chain of thoughts by becoming aware of the gap between them, you can widen the gap and thereby break your attachment to them.

The more you practice this, you will find that the old pre-programmed thoughts that used to plague your awareness die down and are replaced by an entirely new set of thoughts, arising from the Source.

Detaching from Thoughts

Being vigilant is essential to remain detached. When we are not alert, the natural tendency is to identify with our thoughts.

With alertness, we can use thoughts as reminders to focus on Presence instead of focusing on the content of our thoughts.

> During festivals, we see fireworks that light up the night sky. Flares rise up in the sky, create a dazzling display of forms and colous and then die down into the emptiness of the sky.

> The flares can take any shape. It can be a display of a happy smiling face, or even a sad frowning face. You enjoy seeing the fireworks regardless of the form that the flares show in the sky.

Thoughts can be witnessed as flares that arise in the sky of silence. Regardless of the content of your thoughts, you can enjoy the wondrous display that arises in the vast stillness of consciousness.

Who-you-truly-are is permanent, eternal. Thoughts come and go. They are like flares that shoot into the night sky. They appear for some time and then fade away in the sky of consciousness.

By merely watching your thoughts that pass by as a witness, you stop energizing them.

Witness the Tunnel of Negativity

If you've travelled by train, you would have experienced that it becomes dark when the train passes through a tunnel. What do you do when the train passes through the tunnel? Your attention suddenly turns within, as there is nothing to watch outside in the darkness. Your gaze is fixed on the other mouth of the tunnel, where bright daylight appears. You know that it's just a matter of time before you will be out of the darkness of the tunnel in the brightness of daylight.

In the same way, whenever situations that cause negative feelings like sorrow, disappointment, anger, or despair occur, remind yourself:

"I am joy that is travelling through this tunnel of sorrow"

"I am peace travelling through this tunnel of anger"

"I am bright faith, travelling through this tunnel of despair."

You will say so with the firm conviction that this negative feeling is merely a temporary occurrence in the eternity of love, bliss and peace. Your attention will be focused on the brightness of love, bliss, and peace that will shortly unfold when you are out of the tunnel of negativity.

13

Power of Patience
Watch, Wait with Wonder!

In Japan, there lived a young man who aspired to be the greatest martial artist of the land. He considered that he must train with the best instructor to achieve his dream.

The best instructor was one of the greatest Zen masters of his time. He lived many hundred miles away. One day, the young man left home to go study with this great Zen teacher.

After travelling for several days, he arrived at the school and was given an audience with the teacher. "What do you wish to learn from me?" the master asked.

"I want you to teach me your art and help me become one of the best martial artists in the country," the young man replied. "How long must I study?"

"At least ten years," said the master.

The youngster thought, 'Ten years is a long time. I want to get this done sooner. Certainly if I work harder, I can complete this training earlier. He asked the master, "What if I train twice as hard as everyone else? How long would it take then?"

"Then it would take twenty years," replied the master.

This answer surprised the young man. He thought, 'That's even longer! I don't want to spend twenty years learning something! I've got other things to do with my life. Certainly if I toil really hard, I could learn it much quicker'.

So he asked again, "What if I practiced all day and night with all my effort… how long would it take then?"

"Thirty years," was the master's response.

The young student was confused. He wondered how it could take longer if he worked harder. He asked the master "How is that possible? If I work harder, shouldn't I be able to finish earlier? Why would it take longer?"

"Simple. My dear fellow… With one eye focused on your destination, there is only one eye left with which you can find the way. Any endeavour requires effort, but more importantly it also requires patience," said the master.

"Master, I surrender. I accept whatever it will take me to master the art. I am not only willing to be patient, but I will do whatever you say."

"In that case, you can be done in two years!" said the Master with a wry smile.

It is said that good things come to those who wait.

When you hear the word 'patience,' you may assume that all you have to do is set your intention and then sit on your haunches and wait for good things to come flooding in. That's not the case. But, you also don't have to struggle and suffer in order to achieve what you want.

The words 'action' and 'reaction' appear more attractive to people than 'patience'. We are so used to *doing* that we find it difficult to simple *be* – because we're conditioned to believe that always doing something is better, and that it's the only way to achieve anything.

Patience is not a passive trait. It is a powerful dynamic state that can take you through every adversity and guarantee your success.

Suppose that you are trying to break a big rock with a hammer. Although you are repeatedly striking hard with the hammer, the stone doesn't break. You might strike and a chip breaks away but you see little progress. You keep at it, nonetheless. Eventually, when you land the hundredth strike the stone breaks.

Were the earlier ninety-nine hammer strikes in vain? No, those strikes had weakened the stone. The ninety-nine strikes were, in fact, the strikes of patience.

Most people feel that the period when they have to keep patience is a one of boredom. This is because they aren't aware of the wonder that is set into motion when we abide in the stillness of patience.

By patiently allowing things to unfold, you have a golden opportunity to be in the moment, to enjoy the process, to marvel at the miraculous ways things come together, to learn, and to experience being in Presence. Patience gives you the opportunity to experience happiness in both, the process and the result.

Through contemplation and patience, you can un-wrap the hidden gifts and lessons from any situation; you can experience the Presence of the Source.

The Value of Waiting

Some things may require extreme patience. If you sow the seed of black bamboo, then you have to patiently tend to it for several months before the seed even sprouts. But once it sprouts, it grows to the height of thirty feet within just three months! This is the fruit of patience.

Whenever you have to exhibit great patience, remember the black bamboo example – wait long enough, and you will get astonishingly fast results as reward for your patience. For the bamboo to grow staggeringly fast, you must first be patient. Patience is never in vain. All that one has to do is continue taking inspired action, patiently, with persistence.

If your goal is small, then impatience doesn't matter; you can still achieve it even by working impatiently. However, if your goal is grand, then you must be patient and persistent until you achieve it.

In today's 'Instant Era,' we want to acquire everything '*a.s.a.p.*' (as soon as possible). We want to complete too many tasks in a short time. We have become accustomed to impatience, and immediate gratification.

This leads to disappointment. We can never be happy or satisfied, when we have to wait – because many things just cannot manifest instantly in our lives. Not everything we wish for in life happen *a.s.a.p.* Rather they happen in perfect order at the perfect time by '*A.S.P.*' (Abiding in the Source with Patience).

A tree may take many years to grow fully. If you want shade around your house, you must be patient when you plant young saplings. Impatiently dumping fertilizer on the tree to get it to grow faster is counterproductive. The tree will be damaged or killed, by your impatience, and your dream of shade will be either delayed or shattered.

Consider the importance of building a solid foundation for a house. For a long time, it may appear that no progress is being made. It can be frustrating to see your house as a hole in the ground, with nothing much obviously happening. If anything is taking time to manifest in your life, prepare yourself for it while it is being manifested.

We need to consciously wait, to allow the universe to synchronize harmoniously. You know that without a solid foundation, the house will crumble. If you patiently persist, take your time, and give your best effort to building the foundation, then once the foundation is laid, you can build upward very quickly.

Weak roots cannot turn into huge trees. Ill-prepared people live the life of creeping vines and depend upon others for support. If their roots are strong then they can be trees, standing on their own without external support, reaching up to the sky in all their glory.

For example, if you are waiting to manifest a new car, you can perhaps take time to learn to drive, learn about the new car, or clean out your garage to make room for it. In other words, while waiting for things to manifest in life, prepare the space within you to be able to receive it when it arrives. When you raise your receptivity for something, forces are set into motion in the unseen that make it happen.

The magical power of patience can be summed up as, 'Watch, wait with wonder!' The three words, Watch, Wait and Wonder, possess extraordinary power. These words help anchor you in the present moment and prevent you from constantly swinging between past and future. You will get an idea of the power of these words only when you start applying them to your life.

For most people, waiting is agonizing. They cannot stop thinking about the future. They not only miss out on the joy of the moment, but also often ruin things while in the state of restlessness by trying to force things to evolve too quickly. With the help of "Watch, Wait with Wonder," you witness wonders happening during the waiting period.

Most people give the right responses at the wrong time or the wrong responses at the right time. This complicates their life situations. As people do not know when and how much to wait, the problem that was about to be resolved, remains unsolved.

For example, if you are having an argument with your spouse, you may be choosing the wrong responses or the wrong timing due to lack of patience. You may lose your temper and start yelling. You don't have to do this. If you learn the art of waiting and responding at the right time, the argument doesn't have to escalate. You may be tempted to respond impulsively to your spouse's seemingly unacceptable words and try to get back at him or her. Just restrain yourself… be patient… and respond when you have your emotions under control. Your words and actions will then be based on love and not hate.

Learning the art of waiting transforms a reactive way of life into a creative experience.

Develop the ability to take a step back and witness everything. Be aware of your physical reactions, your impulses, emotions and thoughts. If you simply observe how something is making you feel, and give it just a few moments before responding, you will begin to grasp the art of 'responding' rather than 'reacting.'

> When a music composer creates a piece of music, he introduces pauses between the notes. He intuitively senses how long to wait before playing the next note. The pauses between each note lend depth to the music. His intuitive waiting brings harmony to the composition.

Similarly when we become experts at waiting for the right period of time and taking action at the right time, life falls into a beautiful rhythm. It will attune with the highest vibration of the universe.

The Art of Waiting – The Waiting Meditation

Meditation is a practice that teaches patience. The experience of Presence that deepens with the practice of meditation lends wonder, bliss and contentment to every moment of life. The body can be trained to remain still. The mind can be trained to remain focused. Meditation teaches us the art of waiting. Waiting gives us the laser focus necessary to give the correct commands to the universe.

The following meditation, called 'Waiting Meditation', will help you develop the Art of Waiting.

> Sit in a comfortable posture, close your eyes, and observe the stream of thoughts as they arise and subside. Mentally say "Next" with every thought, allowing it to pass. Practice this for some time. You will find that you are able to detach from the stream of thoughts.
>
> With the passage of time, thoughts can become sparse, allowing you to feel in the space between thoughts. This space, though just a brief instant at first, is a period of waiting – waiting for the next thought to arise.
>
> In the waiting state, if a thought arises, let go of it and ask, "Where will my next thought come from?"
>
> Pay attention to the sounds around you. Notice whether the next thought arises from the sounds that you hear? You'll find that thoughts do not arise from the sounds.
>
> Now observe your breath. There's no need to regulate it. Just observe it and seek whether the next thought arises from the breath. Thoughts are not arising from the breath. Just keep observing what's happening.
>
> Observe the pains and sensations in the body. Do thoughts arise from the pains, from the sensations? Does the next thought arise from an ache that you may be experiencing?

Does the next thought arise from any odor that you can sense, or the taste that you are feeling right now on your tongue?

Keep asking, "Where will my next thought come from?" Be intent on knowing the source of the next thought.

Be in this state of unconditional waiting. Keep observing every sensation to see where the next thought comes from. It is not necessary that some thought must arise. Sometimes there will be blissful silence. Wait unconditionally.

In this manner, you will be able to observe everything that is, as it is, without getting entangled in your thoughts.

If a thought arises which announces, "This is boring", just let it pass by and await the source of the next thought.

In this state of unconditional waiting, the truth of your Presence, the truth of the Source will be revealed. Continue to wait unconditionally whether it gets revealed or it doesn't.

Enjoy this state of waiting… a kind of waiting wherein you are welcoming life to happen, waiting for nothing in particular. You do not await any specific outcome. You wait unconditionally.

Open your eyes. Continue in this state of waiting for the next thought for some time with open eyes.

Unconditional waiting helps you break free from the habit of compulsive thinking. You do not allow pain sensations or feelings to draw your attention indiscriminately. By remaining in this state of unconditional waiting, you let go of impulses that you would otherwise chase after. You connect with the Source.

Part III

Living with the Source

Some people seem to have it all, while others are in a constant state of struggle. What is the difference between these people? Is it hard work? Is it about being knowledgeable or learned? Being at the right place at the right time? Being 'born lucky'?

None of these offers complete and satisfactory answers.

Those who grow both spiritually and materially, who are successful, for whom life seems to flow easily, intuitively know and abide by certain universal laws, even if they cannot put them into words.

Just as there are physical laws that govern the world phenomena, there are also laws that work in the mental realm that determine what we create and experience in life. These laws have existed since the beginning of time and precede the appearance of human life. They are unchanging, universal and apply to everyone, without exception. The laws operate relentlessly and impartially, regardless of whether you feel wealthy or deprived, irrespective of whether life seems to be a success or failure.

One who ignores these laws is at risk of driving the vehicle of life without knowledge of its consequences. Instead of trying to *exploit* these laws for personal gains, it is a must to know how to abide by these laws to enact the will of the Source. Simply abiding by these laws can create a life brimming with love, happiness and peace.

When we operate in life, abiding by the Laws of Thought, these laws begin to work for us.

In order to transform our lives, we must be aware of our thoughts and use them wisely. It is in our best interest to contemplate these laws of thought and act deliberately according to their guiding principles, rather than letting them work randomly by unconsciously misdirecting their forces.

This part of the book is about balancing your inner world with life in the external world. It is about understanding how to relate with the nuances of living in the world based on the wisdom of the Source.

The chapters that follow explain how to find congruence between inner spiritual growth and lasting success and fulfillment in the external world.

14

Law of Creation
Manifest qualities, not things

"Build me a war room", said the CEO to the architect who was building him an office. He continued, "Build this room as a shrine for creativity. Put up pictures of creative geniuses and business moguls. Use technology to fill the room with words of great minds and equip it to be able to play the best music ".

"Tell me the objective and leave the means to me", said the architect.

The CEO did not argue since he knew that he was speaking to one of the giants of architecture. "The objective: I want a place to think and create. I should be able to enter this room and clearly see in my mind the problems that ail my company. I should be able to go to war with whatever doesn't work in my company and eliminate it."

"And why would you want to do that?" asked the architect.

"Because, I want to scale heights that no one ever has."

After three months, the CEO was led to his Thinking Room by the architect.

The CEO was astounded by what he saw. It had nothing that he had asked for. But he immediately felt blissful and at peace. The room had no furniture, except for a meditation cushion with a back rest at the centre. The centerpiece of the room was a large white wall with a black dot at the centre. The wall opposite was a massive sliding glass door from where he could look into the expanse of a beautiful garden. The smaller wall to the left was just a large mirror and the one to the right had a water fountain covering the entire wall.

Before he could say anything, the architect said, "Your ultimate objective was to have a place to think and scale heights no one has achieved. But you wanted me to build a room that will help you think and see 'what is'. I have built you one to see 'what isn't'. Only those who go beyond visible problems and envision unseen possibilities can innovate and scale the great heights that you dream of. You wanted a room to go to war with whatever isn't working. Being at peace is what will truly help you surmount the impossible."

"Indeed, I can now see how my ultimate objective will be achieved. I love it! This is amazing. I understand the purpose of the black dot is to remind me to focus on the white space around it. I will surely remember to envision what isn't, not just focus on problems. I can understand the significance of the meditation cushion too. But, please explain the mirror."

"It is to remind you that your world is a mirror. Whatever you see outside is but a reflection of who you are within. You are the source of your world."

"And the open vista into the garden and the water fountain"

"Look through the glass to be reminded of the abundance of resources nature provides you. And the sound of water is the only music you will need for your meditative thinking."

"If this is what you have built for me, I would love to see your office, where you might be fashioning such amazing ideas." said the CEO.

"I have no office. I work from home, in cafes and gardens. I close my eyes in silence to enter my inner office and these designs emerge", replied the architect.

A pile of rocks ceases to be a pile of rocks, the moment one abides in silence, holding within his mind an image of a house. The man doesn't see the pile of rocks for what it is – he sees it for what it isn't, for what it could be–a house. He sees the possibility; therefore, he plants in his mind the seed of creation. Without that seed of creation in his mind, the pile of rocks remains merely a pile of rocks. He would never pick up these rocks and use them to build a house.

We are all creators of our own life experiences. This is according to a universal law, the Law of Creation:

Before anything in this world is created in the physical plane, it is first created from the Source in the mental plane.

This is the fundamental process of creation: you must first think it, in order to experience it; and every creative thought arises from the Source.

You may be used to thinking that life happens to you and you simply react to life. The truth is that your thoughts are immensely powerful. They create your reality and shape your life. Manifested thoughts are how life happens *through* you, not to you.

Imagine a fertile field that represents the field of life. Thoughts are like seeds that fall into this field, sprout and grow to attain their highest potential. The Source is the field that lends life to those thoughts. Whatever thoughts you sow in the field of the Source will manifest. Sow thoughts of poverty and scarcity, and you will manifest poverty, you will experience scarcity. Sow seeds of loneliness into the field, and you will experience loneliness. By the same law, though, if you sow seeds of abundance, success, happiness, love and health into the field of the Source, you cannot help but experience them in your life!

The Source is the ocean of life, from where everything arises, in which everything blossoms, due to which everything is being sustained, and into which everything ultimately dissolves. However, this immense and all-pervading ocean of life shows no judgment. Anything that arises in the Source is enlivened and manifested without bias.

Understanding the Law of Creation

Some people believe that bad things always happen to them despite their best intentions or best efforts. They falter at the finishing line, or never start for fear of failing. When it is their turn at the ticket window, the movie is sold out. Once they understand the power of thoughts and replace their negative thoughts with positive thoughts, they discover that the world begins to support them.

With this type of thinking in place, even when they get to the ticket window at the movie theater and the tickets are sold out, they will experience miracles such as being offered tickets by a stranger who bought them and discovered he can't use them. So, what changed? Merely their way of thinking!

The root cause of our suffering lies in our own method of thinking. Those who recognize the importance of training their minds are the ones who actually undertake the training required to improve not only themselves but the world. Those who don't realize the significance of this training run away from it by offering excuses.

In fact, it's just as simple to choose a positive thought as it is to choose a negative thought. It takes practice to re-program our habitual negativity, but we can do it, and the results will be nothing short of miraculous!

The Law of Creation is not just about positive thinking. It is about understanding that everything arises from your thoughts, which originate from the universal creative potential of the Source. The significance of this is to understand that if everything is created first in the mental realm from the Source, then it is important to create consciously, with a positive purposeful intention.

Before we dive into how this creative potential can be unleashed in our lives, let us look at the science behind the Law of Creation.

Revelations from Quantum Physics

You may be astounded at just how powerful your thoughts are. The thoughts that draw your attention are commands to the universal creative potential of the Source.

Scientists, too, have begun to acknowledge the importance and the power of the Laws of Thought. Revelations from research in the field of quantum physics have revolutionized our perspective of the essence of wholeness and the illusion of matter.

Quantum physicists discovered that physical atoms are made up of spinning energy. Each atom is like a spinning top that radiates energy.

Scientists observed that when observed from a distance, atoms appear like translucent spheres. As they dug deeper, they noticed that the atom is empty. The atom disappears! What appeared as the structure of the atom turns out to be physical emptiness when scrutinized deeply.

They concluded that atoms are made of invisible energy, not tangible matter. It then appears that all material substance in the universe is actually energy vibrating in physical emptiness.

Further, quantum physicists inferred that matter could be simultaneously defined as a material particle as well as an immaterial energy field – a wave. Albert Einstein realized and concluded with his famous equation: $E = mc^2$, that energy and matter are one and the same. Einstein discovered that the universe that we live in is not made up of discrete, material objects separated by space. The universe is one indivisible, dynamic whole. Energy and matter are aspects of the same underlying unified field.

Physicists performed an experiment of passing electrons through a double-slit. When an electron wave was made to pass through the double-slit and fall upon a photographic film, it created a pattern of striations, indicating wave-interference. This suggested that the electrons were behaving like waves (energy). However, when scientists tried to observe the electron, they were baffled to find that it *chose* a particular slit, as if it were a particle.

When scientists attempted to watch electron behavior, the observed outcome of experiments was influenced by what they expected to see!

John Von Neumann and Eugene Wigner have postulated their interpretation of Heisenberg and Schrodinger's experiments. Their interpretation is summarized as follows:

> The behavior of a system upon observation is completely different than its usual behavior: The wave-function that describes a system spreads out into an ever larger superposition of different possible situations. However, during observation, the wave-function describing the system collapses to one of several options. If there is no observation, this collapse does not occur, and none of the options ever become less likely.

> The rules of quantum mechanics are correct but there is only one system which may be treated with quantum mechanics, namely the entire material world. There exist external observers which cannot be treated within quantum mechanics, namely human minds, which perform measurements causing wave-function collapse.

So what does that mean for us? The implications are enormous.

- An observer actually modifies objective outcomes simply by the act of observation. In other words, we shape our world by the way we observe it.

- When not observed, everything exists as a field of infinite possibilities, collapsing into a particular manifestation when observed.

The observer exists beyond the manifested world. The observer field is like a screen projecting the material manifestation upon itself, just as a movie is projected on a cinema screen. Thus, at the level of wholeness, intelligence exists which *observes* the world into existence.

Everything is first created from the Source in the mental plane. From these experiments, it can be concluded that –

The Source is your essential nature that observes and participates in the creative process through the medium of your thoughts.

Creation From the Source

Everything you focus on—good or bad—will eventually manifest in your life. Whatever thoughts or feelings you give your attention to, is like placing an order for more of the same. It's important, then, to direct your energy to positive feelings and on what you want, instead of negative feelings of fear or worry about what you don't want.

Happiness is a powerful catalyst that fuels the process of manifestation. Being in pure causeless happiness empowers your thoughts and guarantees their manifestation, provided they are imbued with purity of purpose.

Let's say you are feeling low and dejected due to a particular situation. Instead of going down a negative spiral, you may consciously choose to respond positively by saying "I may be feeling low, but my future is bright and promising. Everything changes with time. This too shall change."

But when you check within yourself, you discover that underneath this positive thinking lies a negative feeling that keeps pulling you: "While I know that I need to focus on the positive side, I'm still in this situation that I cannot escape from." This subtle negative pull has an impact on you, and you don't even realize it!

You may ask, "How can I think positively when I am gripped by such negativity? How do I generate positive thoughts when I am surrounded by negative energy? Even though I think positively, I'm not able to sustain it for long. How do I release the grip of negative feelings?"

Positive thinking is certainly better than negative thinking, but a new dimension is necessary.

Creating from the happy natural state of the Source is a new paradigm that takes you beyond both positivity and negativity, beyond polarities. It helps you see people, incidents, and life from a perspective beyond the positive and the negative.

We are essentially the limitless expanse of the Source. We can therefore manifest the qualities of the Source when and where we want. The trouble is that we look at manifestation as bringing forth more money or more comforts in our lives. We shall now understand how manifesting the overarching qualities of the Source, actually takes care of all our needs.

For example, when you find that you desire a good bank balance, your actual overarching desire is for abundance. So then, you choose to manifest abundance from the Source, not just a good bank balance. The bank balance is already a part of the abundance that you create from the Source.

If you are troubled by differences in relationships, then instead of desiring a resolution to these differences, you rather manifest peace, which is the quality of the Source.

You create from the Source by first accessing the happy natural state of the Source. With this, you move beyond the particular desire and focus on manifesting the overarching quality of the Source.

Express gratitude for the particular quality of the Source that you wish to manifest. Expressing gratitude by being in the pure presence of the Source, takes you beyond both positivity and negativity. A powerful way to access and create from the Source is to heartily say "Thank You" for the qualities of the Source already present within you and also within everyone.

Express gratitude to the qualities of the Source instead of focusing on limitations. The shining sun, an abundant harvest, cleanliness, an act of compassion, are only but a few expressions of the myriad qualities of the Source. These are obvious manifestations of consciousness.

The Key to Manifestation From the Source

There are three steps to creating from the Source:

Step 1: Decide what you would like to create

Depending on the situation, decide the overarching quality of the Source that you would intend to create.

For instance, if you would like more money to solve a problem, intend to create abundance. Positive thinking is about manifesting money. Transcend this and instead decide to create abundance.

If you have had an argument with your spouse, do not merely intend, "I wish my spouse becomes a better person" Instead ask yourself, what is the quality of the Source you would like to be filled with? You would like to manifest love and peace.

For recovering from ill-health, you may want to bring forth the qualities of harmony and peace.

Some of the qualities of the Source you may want to manifest are: Love, Joy, Peace, Harmony, Compassion, Consistency, Abundance, Creativity, Patience, Courage, Detachment, Communicativeness.

Step 2: Connect to the Source

Use any of the methods such as "Thought Numbering", "Happy Thought", "Good Morning Peace", "Next", "I am", "Who am I now?", or "A-B-C-D" explained earlier to access the Source.

Step 3: Repeatedly tell yourself, "Thank you for _____"

For a few minutes, repeat in your mind the quality of the Source you have decided to create in Step 1. You may want to express gratitude to two qualities in the given situation. So you could say, "Thank you for love and peace." It is helpful if you stick to maximum two or three qualities so that you can fully bring forth that quality into manifestation. When you are in the peaceful presence of the Source, you can bring forth the feeling of whatever you wish to create, be it love, or joy or peace.

When you say "Thank You," you send a signal to the Universe that you see only the truth of the Source. Then the Universe rallies behind you and the qualities of the Source begin to work through you. As your feelings change you know that change has begun to manifest.

How does this take you beyond the positive and the negative? If you are grateful about 'everything in life', you automatically move away from doubts, worries, and feelings of scarcity. When you are present in gratitude, you automatically and constantly focus on the best; and therefore, you will receive the best!

Gratitude makes you receptive to the unfolding of your highest possibilities. Gratitude removes the feelings of fear and worry that come with the belief of scarcity and competition. For example: instead of complaining that it's raining, enjoy the life-giving moisture. Instead of grumbling about facing a new challenge, focus on the success waiting beyond it.

When individuals indulge in negative thinking, they're unaware of the truth that is waiting to unfold, the qualities of the Source that await expression. They can't see past the deluding scenes. The illusory truth grips their attention. This lack of clear vision blocks new and exciting possibilities from manifesting in their lives.

The Source expresses itself as harmony, peace, love, joy and abundance through us. This is the nature of the Source. When we happily thank the Source in full faith for bringing forth the quality we would like to create, we are seeing fulfillment as already given. This is the most powerful way of creating a perfect life from the Source.

15

Law of Direction
Catalyze the creative process

The famed Indian cricketer, M.A.K. Pataudi, had suffered an accident in which he lost an eye at the age of twenty-one.

Even though he realized that he had virtually lost the use of one eye, he never considered that he might not be able to play cricket again. He refused to believe that he was done with the game.

His passion for the game saw him back in the nets within a month after his surgery. He braved the limitation that the impaired vision had brought him in daily life with the clear intention of getting back into the game. The loss of one eye leads to a loss in visual perspective and judgment of depth. Yet, he persisted in his chosen direction of getting his batting right. He practiced for long hours.

In his words, "At first I couldn't pick the length of the bowling at all. Then I reached a sort of compromise, but I suppose it took five years before I could claim to be completely on terms with my handicap."

His passion and persistent intent brought him back into international cricket, where he went on to become one of India's most successful cricket captains.

The question most people ask immediately upon learning about the Law of Creation is: If things are first created in the realm of thoughts before they are brought into reality, does every thought that I think, manifest into reality?

Every thought that occurs does impact life in some way, but not every thought manifests automatically. Castles built in air remain figments of our imagination. Every stray thought that we entertain, need not manifest.

The only thoughts that will transform themselves into physical reality are those that are consciously directed, and have both awareness and passion associated with them.

This is why it is important to understand the Law of Direction:

> ### *When you direct your thoughts consciously and passionately, they manifest.*

This law can be broken down into two aspects:

- The first is that you must be conscious of the thoughts that arise from the Source. In order for them to manifest in your physical reality, you must hold them in your mind with awareness and direct them with clarity.

- The second aspect of the law deals with the power of feelings. Only those thoughts that are powered by your passion and intention actually manifest.

We've all daydreamed about the future to some extent. Perhaps you began, as many individuals do, with thoughts similar to: "I want this. I will do this when such a thing happens. Then this is what will happen next and then..."

There's a reason why such stray thoughts do not take root and grow. You may be unconsciously working against your own wishes. If you think that your desires are not manifesting at all, you need to contemplate whether your thoughts are canceling each other out.

A person thinks, "How I wish there were peace at home." The Law of Creation sets the thought into manifestation. His mind begins to attract things in his life that will make him more peaceful. But the very next day, or perhaps even the very next hour, he thinks, "Peace will never be possible in this house. My wife is such a difficult person. She makes it impossible; she'll never change."

His second thought has neutralized the impact that his first thought would have had on his situation. Though he wants peace, his thoughts have cancelled one another out. He doesn't realize how costly that one negative thought will be, and he'll not enjoy the fruits of his positive thoughts in these circumstances.

This makes it essential to think clearly. It is crucial not to entertain the notion that peace is not possible. If you want a home that is permanently peaceful, you can indeed attain it as long as another thought does not interfere with it. It is vital to be aware of your thoughts and direct them towards attaining a life of love, joy, health, wealth and peace.

The moment you think a clear thought, you begin to attract everything needed to fulfill that thought. The power of your feelings then acts as a catalyst to hasten this process.

Because the Law of Creation works invisibly, man forgets to lend his thoughts the power of passion. He complains that whatever he intended never comes to fruition. Thinking something once and then moving onto something else is not enough. Hold the thought in your awareness. Follow it up with passion and conscious intention.

With strong intent, you must passionately believe what you desire will manifest. Repeated contemplation generates the necessary feeling of passion. In order for the intensity of your thought to be magnified, your mind must be clear. You must be serious about your intent, and you must be sure not to treat it as simply another stray thought.

What you passionately feel about is what makes a difference. Conversely, when you hold negative feelings about what you want to attract into your life, you are pushing what you want further away from you and keep it from happening. If, for example, you constantly worry about money while intending to become wealthy, the negative feeling will supersede your positive thought.

Thus, if the Law of Creation teaches you to manifest the overarching qualities of the Source instead of focusing on the material aspects, the Law of Direction further guides you not to worry about material things in your day to day life too.

Returning to the example of differences with your spouse, when you get some time in solitude, you decide to apply the Law of Creation. You close your eyes and repeatedly tell yourself, "Thank you for Love and Peace" till you begin to feel the love and peace by being in the experience of the Source.

After opening your eyes, when you interact with your spouse, do not again get worked up if (s)he does not respond the way you would like. Even if (s)he were to say something that you perceive not to be loving, continue to harbour love and peace in your heart.

Do not change the direction of your thoughts or alter your feelings. If required, you may mentally keep saying, "Thank you for Love and Peace."

Whatever You Resist Will Persist

Many people strongly feel that their co-workers should not disturb them. They are focused on the thought that people at work should not trouble them. The more they hold such a negative thought, they often seem to find people bothering them while they are trying to work. In other words, they get what they do *not* want because of the power of negative feelings that they entertain. Instead, these individuals should feel passionately about the kind of people they would prefer to be surrounded with.

Similarly, if you want to be at your ideal weight, don't feel let down about being obese. Feel passionate about the activities that you can engage in when your body has an ideal weight; feel passionate about how light and fit you would feel.

Create what you want from the Source in your thoughts and feelings and do not change the direction of your thoughts once you have set the manifestation process in motion. Persist with the direction of your thoughts even if the situations around you may be presenting a contradictory picture.

> Suppose you wish to manifest justice and equality at your workplace through your thoughts and feelings. However, if you see your boss treating some employees unfairly, do not start cursing him and nullifying what you have begun to manifest.

> You can instead feel grateful for the incident that it teaches you how NOT to treat employees…it opens your heart to the pain that your boss feels within (hurtful actions are never borne of love). In this way, in spite of an undesirable situation, your thoughts do not change course.

When What You Desire Does Not Manifest…

When we find that what we desire doesn't seem to be manifesting, we tend to lose hope and give up abiding by these principles. Our thoughts begin to vacillate between what we want and the contradictory scenes that we are experiencing.

When we vacillate between positive and negative thoughts, the results also keep fluctuating – sometimes favorably, sometimes unfavorably. We should refrain from sowing seeds of negativity in our minds. Everything is first created in thoughts but it gains momentum with passion and enthusiasm.

Sometimes, you may find that results of what you have wished for are not coming your way, even though you were very clear in your thoughts. Your awareness and clarity of thoughts do attract the results towards you, but they struggle to reach you because you haven't empowered your thoughts with enough enthusiasm.

Since all this is invisible, you don't realize that the results have stopped midway. Tired of waiting, you stop empowering your thoughts. For example, suppose in the pursuit of health you take positive steps like exercising well, eating only healthy food, praying and meditating. But if you become discouraged due to a minor illness and stop infusing your mind with enthusiasm, the health that was on its way to you, halts in its tracks.

When things don't go the way you would like them to, it does not mean that nature is saying 'NO'; it only means that nature is saying 'NOT NOW'. Take courage from this truth. At this juncture, there is nothing to be done. It is time to rest in the Presence of the Source.

When desires do not seem to be manifesting, it is time to invoke the Power of Patience. With patience, you can happily tide through every adversity and guarantee your success.

By patiently allowing things to unfold, you abide in the present moment and enjoy the process. This becomes possible when you practice the meditations for resting in the experience of the Source. You witness the scenes that unfold with detachment and wonder at the miraculous ways that things come together. In the process, you learn to be in Presence of the Source.

Patience teaches us to rejoice not only when we attain what we desire, but also during the process leading to it.

16

Law of Focus
Be clear about what you want

A wealthy merchant had amassed many diamonds over the years from his business earnings. He used to always anxiously think, 'I have worked so hard to earn these diamonds. My diamonds should not be stolen. No thief should eye my wealth.' He worried about the safety of his precious diamonds, anxious that it should not be stolen.

This merchant had a son who had travelled far and wide. He had collected many unique, rare and priceless artifacts during his travels. It was his dream to build a museum to display his collection of relics so that visitors could enjoy and marvel at them. The boy used to thank God and pray, 'Dear Lord, I have collected all these rare artifacts from far and wide. I like each and every one of these. These articles must always remain safe with me.'

There was a burglar in the same town. Since the past many days, he was constantly held with a thought, 'I have done many petty thefts; now it's time to go for a big kill so that I can join the league of big crooks and gain clout and respect in my fraternity of thieves.'

The local police inspector used to often think, 'I have captured many small time crooks. I need to now catch a notorious criminal and solve a big case of theft, so that I can get promoted. Then I will become a hero and be the talk of the town.'

The merchant's wife wished, 'It has been quite a while since I have visited my parents. May be I should go visit them for few days. It will be good for me to get a break from this daily grind.'

In this situation, let us now see how their diverse thoughts functioned according to the Laws of Thought for each one of them.

The thief soon started scouting the affluent localities of the town. He surveyed the mansions of wealthy people and spotted the merchant's mansion. He thought that the merchant's mansion looked posh and a soft target for looting all the wealth stashed inside.

One night, as per plan, the thief committed the burglary at the merchant's mansion. He broke open the safe and robbed the merchant of all his jewels, diamonds and money. He managed to successfully escape from the scene of crime. It was surprising that the thief did not touch a single artifact that belonged to the merchant's son.

After the theft, the merchant was grief-stricken. He had lost his zeal for life. His worst fears had come true. Out of agony, he pleaded, "Oh Lord, I always revered you and undertook so many religious rituals to please you. Is this how you reward me?! I want my wealth back."

The case of this robbery was assigned to the Inspector who had dreamed of catching a big criminal. Soon the police inspector caught the thief *and earned himself the fame and promotion that he had dreamed of.*

In the meanwhile, the merchant had to spend time in court proceedings and follow-up with the police to conclude the case. As he could hardly be at home, he sent his wife off to visit her parents.

This story reveals the secret of the power of focus in manifesting whatever you wish for in your life. Take a moment and contemplate on it.

There are five characters in this story. They all prayed for different things. The merchant wished that his diamonds shouldn't be stolen. His son wished that his priceless artifacts should always remain safe with him so that people could enjoy seeing them. The thief had only one thought, 'I want to rob a very wealthy person so that I belong in the league of big robbers'. The Inspector wished to solve a big case and catch a notorious thief so that he could get promoted. The merchant's wife wanted to visit her parents for a few days. All their prayers were manifested in accordance with their wishes.

Now, let's look at the secret of this story. The key thing to understand in the story is that the merchant should have focused on what he wanted, rather than focusing on what he did not want.

From the first two laws, it is clear that you can create what you want from the Source. Once you decide what you want to create from the Source, do not change the direction of your thoughts and feelings.

But then, what is it that you *really* want?

Your thoughts are more powerful than you can imagine. The thoughts that you keep are, in reality, orders you're giving the universe. In response, the universe creates situations, events and circumstances accordingly.

The media constantly bombards us with information about the next swanky car, the latest gadgets, the next high paying job or client. This includes the Internet, television, newspapers, radio, to name just a few of the channels. Indirectly or directly, these channels of information play a vital role in shaping our thinking on various issues. It dictates not just what we should desire, but also how we should interpret the world.

Negative content expressed by the media makes viewers believe the world to be a dangerous, hopeless and miserable place. If we carefully scrutinize the effects of television on society, we find that indiscriminate viewers look at the world with skepticism. They tend to form skewed opinions and develop self-limiting attitudes. For example, millions of individuals worldwide are actually giving harmful orders to the universe. Their negative focus is like saying, "War is inevitable; crime is on the rise; peace is impossible; terrorism will stay…"

People need to learn that they must stop giving the universe erroneous orders based on what they read or hear. Similarly, the members of the media must learn the potency of their words, given the tendency of many in these communities to sensationalize facts.

Contrary to what many individuals may believe, nothing in life comes to us out of the blue. Incidents in our lives occur based on the commands we have given to the universe through our thinking. If we experience hatred and vengeance in our lives, it is a result of our own orders.

This knowledge may come as a surprise to you. There certainly are many who would choose not to believe this. They question how they could be responsible for the negative incidents in their lives. But the truth of the matter is that the main reason for negative results is unconscious negative thinking and a negative focus in life. If one focuses on what they don't want, then they'll end up getting precisely that.

We have already understood from the experiments of Quantum Physics, described earlier, that an observer actually modifies objective outcomes in his world. What we expect to observe actually shapes our world. Our attention directs our energies. Wherever attention goes, energy flows.

The Law of Focus states:

> ***Focus on what you really want,***
> ***not on what you don't want.***

There are two aspects to this law, focusing on what you really want and not focusing on what you don't want.

Focus on What You Truly Want

First, you need to be clear about what you truly want. Everything that you desire ultimately points to the yearning for lasting love, happiness and peace. The power of love, happiness and peace springs from the Source. They already exist within us.

People are generally unaware of their true desires. The first step is to understand our true deeper needs. If we become aware of what we truly need, then Love, Joy and Peace are bound to make way in our lives.

Whatever you want already exists; all that remains is for it to be manifested. When you know this, you can choose to be happy, here and now. If you wait for an external *reason* to be happy and say, "I shall be happy only when this particular wish is fulfilled," then you may wait forever.

Apply the Law of Focus by contemplating on every desire and linking it to the higher qualities of Love, Joy and Peace.

Do Not Focus on What You Don't Want

The second aspect of the Law of Focus is to *not* focus on what you don't want.

Refrain from focusing your attention on the kind of people you do *not* want in your life. Instead, focus on the kind of people you want to attract in your life –people who help you grow spiritually, who raise your consciousness, and who assist your progress towards your life goals. Stop thinking, "Why is this person in my life? What did I do to have such people around me? Why me? When will such people go away?"Remember, negative events, people, or situations you resist, will persist.

The advice given to those who are sick is, "Be at ease to be free from disease."Usually, those who are sick are focusing on their illness - the pain, the struggle, and the discomfort. Instead, they should focus on having perfect health: "I am in perfect health; I take care of my body with the right nutrition, daily exercise and adequate quality sleep; I enjoy vitality and wellbeing."

The more one focuses on sickness, the more it persists. Stop commanding the universe to keep you sick with thoughts such as: "When will my illness go away? What have I done to deserve this? I hope I don't develop a chronic disease. Will I ever get rid of this obesity?"

When you say to yourself, "I hope I don't get cancer," your focus is entirely on cancer, instead of health. This may seem like such a small error in your thinking. However, it can lead to disastrous consequences. People focus on what they don't want and end up attracting just that.

The moment you focus your attention on what you want and stop giving attention to what you don't want, the latter begins to diminish from your life. If there are people in your life that are bad influences, or those that you don't like, don't think about getting them out of your life. Just focus on what kind of people you *do* want around you.

In order to attract such people, pray, "I am surrounded by loving and happy people." or "My life is full of love, joy and peace."Automatically, those who do not fit these criteria will disappear from your life or change the way they behave towards you.

Are You Focusing on Negativity Indirectly?

You may say, "I never intended negative situations for myself, then why am I getting these results now?" No one ever intends negative outcomes, yet unconsciously you may be giving negative commands without realizing it. You may not have directly thought that an accident should happen to you, but every time someone else had an accident, you may have thought, "I hope this doesn't happen to me." Whether you realize it or not, your focus within that statement is on the negative, and the Universe considers that as an order to be manifested.

Why? Because the subconscious mind cannot picture the word 'No'. If you tell the mind *not* to think of a green monkey, it *will* think of a green monkey. If you tell the mind that you don't like terrorists or terrorism, the picture in your mind is that of terrorists and terrorism.

When a mother tells a child, "Don't bang the door," the picture created in the child's mind is that of a door being banged. Instead, she should tell the child, "Can you close the door gently?" Positive language is essential for proper upbringing of children.

This is not just true for children. It's true for everyone. Advertisers use this principle to their advantage. They say, "Don't buy this car till you test drive it." The picture being imprinted in the minds of the audience is to go and buy the car. While advertisers are aware of this rule of the mind, many government bodies are ignorant of it. That's why you see huge billboards on the road that say: Don't drink and drive. As a result, thousands of minds register the thought of drinking while driving!

You might not be giving negative commands directly, but may still be doing so indirectly. The following example illustrates this point:

A man was given a large vase as a gift, which he displayed in his hall. The vase was quite large and he would often lament that it took up so much space. One day, the vase broke. If you asked the man about it, he would've said, "I never intended that it should break. Why would I want a loss?" You can now understand that he made it happen – indirectly though.

It's a universal law that you'll receive evidence of what you believe. Let's say you believe job interviews are difficult. You'll keep finding yourself in difficult interview situations! It's quite possible you won't ever have a successful interview because of this notion. This notion reinforces your belief that job interviews are tough, and that those who get selected are just lucky. Because of this belief, you may stop preparing for interviews and fail to achieve success. These results will only further affirm and strengthen your belief.

The circle of negativity keeps expanding when those around you, believe you and accept your thinking. What occurs, in effect, is that you're supporting each other's mistaken beliefs. But with awareness and diligence, you can change your beliefs by following the Law of Focus.

Use of "So That"

If a negative thought ever arises in your mind or in your speech, you can add "so that" to neutralize that thought or to turn it into a positive one. For example, instead of saying, 'I want freedom' if you say, 'I don't want bondage' then the latter would happen. Hence, adding 'so that' is important. Now the same negative sentence would be, 'I don't want bondage, *so that* I can enjoy freedom, love, joy and peace.'

When you add "so that" to negative thoughts, it neutralizes their power. The phrase that follows "so that" helps to make your core thought behind the negative thought clearer. Make sure you add a quality of the Source such as love, joy or peace after the phrase "so that..." By adding "so that" to otherwise seemingly negative thoughts or statements, they help you focus on the quality of the Source.

By adding 'so that', you are forced to contemplate why you are demanding something. With this clarity, with every desire, you move towards the Source.

For instance, 'I want to keep my child away from bad company, *so that* she spreads love, joy and peace in society.' Adding "so that" to a thought or a sentence forces you to deeply contemplate, which in turn helps in linking your desire to the Source.

Look at every area of your life and examine whether you're focusing your attention on something negative or something you don't want. If you're focusing on the negative qualities of others, even that is considered a command to the universe and you will simply attract more people with those negative qualities!

The next law explains the flip-side of the Law of Focus. It explains how the world mirrors back what we hold within our minds.

17

———

Law of Resonance
See yourself through the world

One day all the employees reached the office and they saw a big advice displayed at the entrance door which read:

"The person who has been hindering your growth in this company has passed away yesterday. We invite you to join in funeral prayers being offered in a section of the gym."

To start with, they all were saddened as they reflected on the death of one of their colleagues. But after a while, they were curious to know who that person was, who had hindered their growth and that of the company.

As people began to crowd around the coffin, the excitement heightened. Everyone was wondering, "Who is this person who was hindering my progress?"

One after the other, the curious employees lined up to catch a glimpse of who it was. Whoever looked inside was rendered speechless. It was as if someone had touched the deepest part of their soul.

There was a mirror inside the coffin. Each person who looked inside was startled to see their own reflection.

They were angered, considering that it was a foul joke. But then, they calmed down when they read the message that was placed next to the mirror. It read:

"There is only one person who is capable of setting limits to your growth. It is YOU.

You are the only person who can transform your life. You alone can influence your happiness and your success. You are the only one who can help yourself.

Your life does not change when your boss changes, or when your friends change. Your life is not waiting for your parents or partner to change. Your life changes when YOU change. When you go beyond your limiting beliefs and realize that you are the only one responsible for your life.

The most important relationship you can have is the one you have with yourself. Examine yourself. Don't be afraid of difficulties or losses. Be a winner; shape your reality by shaping yourself."

You now know that positive outcomes are a result of your positive orders and the negative because of your negative orders. While that's true, you may be surprised to learn that some of the events you view as negative are really the results of your higher orders –your positive thoughts.

For example, if you've given a command that you intend your career to be successful in a short period, you very well may be confronted with a series of challenges in order for this to happen. When you did not know this, you would have probably viewed these growing pains and the stress related to them as negative.

In reality, they have appeared because of your prayers –your higher orders. In this case, they are part of your orders for a rapidly successful career. There are skills, knowledge and experiences you must have, and you must change the way you view things before you succeed in your career. Challenging situations appear in your life in order to impart you with higher qualities and virtues.

In this way, everything, every setback, frustration, challenge, obstacle or struggle becomes a powerful teacher, a mysterious gift, and an elevating springboard. This understanding in itself will help you access the Source and entertain only happy thoughts even in the midst of terrible struggles.

It immensely helps to be constantly aware that your life situations resonate with the choices you make. Every trial, every situation in life that seems to be painful or frustrating, has been consciously or unconsciously chosen by you in your past, so as to enable you to mature and learn vital lessons –lessons of tenacity, patience, perseverance, compassion, and being in harmony with life itself.

No incident or situation is a problem by itself. A situation is a situation as-is. It becomes a so-called problem or triggers blame or complaint within us only because we are viewing it through the filters of our limiting beliefs.

This is according to the Law of Resonance, which states:

The world is not as it appears to you; the world is how you are.

Beliefs are like roofs. A roof cannot stand by itself; it needs pillars. The roof of belief needs pillars of evidence. If it doesn't have those pillars, it will collapse. The more evidence you acquire, the more pillars you're providing for the roof of the belief, the stronger it becomes. *You get evidences for whatever you choose to believe.*

Given enough time, a strange thing happens. The roof of belief becomes so strong that it doesn't require the pillars of evidence any longer. It stands on its own. In effect, the belief has become your indisputable truth.

This is how the world mirrors how you are: if you're unhappy that people are not helping you, then your belief that people are not helpful gets reflected as evidences in your world. It could also mean that somewhere you are not helping yourself. If people are rude to you, it does not necessarily mean that you are rude to others, but it may mean that your belief that others are rude is causing incidents where people are rude to you repeatedly.

The following scenario occurs every day in classrooms. Students are calm and orderly for one teacher, yet they bring the roof down in another teacher's class. The key is not inherent in the thinking of the students, but in how the teacher thinks and deals with herself. The first teacher listens to herself. Automatically, as the world is a mirror, others listen to her. The second teacher is likely to be someone who does not believe in herself. So, automatically, others do not take her seriously.

How does *your* world resonate with you?

Your world is a screen upon which you project your own mental traits, your unresolved emotions, your strengths and deficiencies. What you view as the world is, in reality, a reflection of what you project.

Have you ever wondered why different people act to the same events in sometimes vastly different ways?

That's because they're projecting or *superimposing* their own mental baggage onto the screen, then watching the scene through their own mental filters. When they do this, it distorts the picture of reality.

We have forgotten that we are the authors of our own reality. Whatever gets 'published' as the visible world is that which we have envisioned and held in our minds.

There is no absolute world *out there*. Rather, you are constantly shaping your own personalized world as you go through life. People, situations, the weather –everything you experience –are shaded by your perception and are projections of what is held deep within your mind.

You mould the personalities of people around you through your own beliefs and assumptions. This occurs without your awareness, and you may probably find yourself criticizing people for shortcomings that are merely a projection of your own beliefs. You experience your own unresolved emotions by unknowingly projecting them on people. So, when someone seems to be angry or deceitful to you, he or she is actually reflecting the anger or deceit which is unresolved within you!

THE SOURCE • 170

What happens in the outside world is a reflection – a perfect resonance – *of what is happening within you. Everything around you resonates with what's going on within your mind.*

This may seem a bit farfetched to believe in the beginning, but when you experiment with this law, you will see how this law has been infallibly functioning. Though it may seem unbelievable, you're actually attracting situations and people into your daily life according to the emotions, traits, and deficiencies you harbor within your mind. You are lost in external details to such an extent that you don't realize these details are only living pictures of what lies buried within your mind.

External situations are not the cause, but rather a reflection *of what you hold within.*

Let's take an example. Suppose it is raining and you hate rains. Rain is simply water falling from the sky. However, your reality is more than just information; it is your experience shaded by your perception. Your perception of the information creates your experience, or your reality. The experience of your world is the result of your perception and interaction with information.

You may sulk and complain about a rainy day but do you ever consider *why* you believe a rainy day to be worthy of a bad mood? Or is it based on some past impression or conditioning? "These rains are so irritating. How they pour water on my plans!" is your *perception* and *interpretation*.

If rain makes you angry, it could be because of your past impressions: perhaps it ruined a special day at the park, or you remember the time your basement was flooded. It could even be from past conditioning–maybe your parents always disliked the rain because the children came home with muddy shoes.

Try comparing your negative interpretation of rain to a farmer's. A farmer may love the rain and be ecstatic that his crops are being watered! It's a matter of perception and context.

Now consider…is one of you wrong and the other right? Of course not! Each person's reality is 100% real, true and valid to them and it depends on their individual context and conditioning.

If one person at a party feels that it's a fun group of people full of stimulating conversation and another person finds the party boring, it's a matter of perception. It's the same party, same people, but two different experiences!

The fascinating thing about your reality is that *you can change it.* You can release yourself from your perspective by being aware that your reality is only *a* reality, not *the only* reality. See your reality as one possible way of perceiving things.

When you drop your preconceived perspectives and access the Source, you become open to this. If you're not aware of your perspective, it can dictate your attitude and your experience.

The Power of Loving Acceptance is the key to transcend the limiting beliefs that resonate as your world. To release the beliefs that you have held within, you need to first bring them to light and accept them completely. Heal all such deep-seated impressions through the practice of forgiveness. Love the part of the world that appears faulty.

If you have anger within you, you will see and hold others as the reason for making you angry. You will also tend to see more anger in others, and believe that they are unnecessarily angry toward you when it's not your fault. The truth is that you're angry with yourself, so you view others as being angry or as the cause of your anger.

Here's another example. If one keeps complaining that other people are not committed, it could possibly mean that somewhere the person is not committed to himself. Since a lack of commitment is an issue from within, the person projects and complains that most people aren't committed. There are leaders who command respect, love, and commitment from people. This is because these leaders are committed to themselves. They do not lack commitment. As a result, they do not see a lack of commitment in others; automatically people are committed to them.

How to Look at the World?

You can utilize the way the world appears to you as a mirror to think deeply about the inner workings of your own mind. It is meant for you to look within yourself, to learn more about how you are actually creating your own life situations through the way you think.

If you can develop an understanding and become aware of the projection that is constantly occurring in your daily life situations, you can actually use these situations to recognize the distortions that are present within your mind. You can then be open to the possibility of clearing such distortions that may exist in your perspective.

For example, if you are engrossed in some urgent or important work, you do not pay much attention to people around you. That does not mean that you do not like them. But if someone else does the same to you, you may misinterpret their actions and make up a story that they are ignoring you and don't like you. This fallacy takes root in your mind and causes unhappiness within you.

In their ignorance, people create such stories from childhood, and sometimes carry them throughout their lives. These stories vary according to their environment and their upbringing. They live their entire lives based upon these make-believe stories.

These stories are the foundation of your thought framework. Often, at the root, there are just a few stories. They are the base on which the rest of your thinking, conclusions, actions and even experiences are based.

Imagine the power that the breaking of even one such story can bring. It can pierce an entire family of thoughts and perceptions based on it, which were unknown to you. The results can be so dramatic that in many cases you won't even know how you became free from the grip of certain vices or habits that had bound you.

Introspection can reveal these underlying stories that the mind has held deeply since childhood. The moment these stories are clearly brought to light, they are automatically replaced by a clearer undistorted view of the world. This way, you can raise yourself beyond the limitations of your past conditioning.

Without understanding this law, you can easily pass judgment about an incident, or a person, without knowing the reality. By truly understanding the Law of Resonance, you can give up this habit of judging and taking your interpretation of an event as the undisputed truth. You will be amazed by the fact that all the events that were the cause of your suffering have become the cause of your joy.

The Law of Resonance implies that you should not focus on the faults of others. Instead, look within. You already know from the understanding of the Law of Focus that the more you focus on faults in the external world, the more faults you will get to see.

To attain our highest potential, we must first get rid of our flaws. We must begin by refusing to focus on the faults of others. *The real fault lies in the blaming eye that sees faults in the world.* Our focus on those faults - meaning the fact that we notice them in the external world – is a reflection of a part of our own inner world. This gives us the opportunity to improve ourselves.

When resistance to something builds within you, when you have constant complaints about something, you become like bronze – lifeless, not attracting the positive aspects. You want to be a magnet that attracts the highest possibilities into your life. But if you focus on the negative, you become non-magnetic. Instead of complaining, give your attention to what you want to see.

When you truly comprehend the world as a mirror, then this understanding enables you to give your attention precisely to what you want to create in your life, instead of focusing on the faults of others.

Whatever you see in the world is telling you the truth about yourself. Otherwise, how will you know yourself? *The eye needs a mirror to see itself.* Similarly, a person needs a mirror in the form of relationships and incidents to recognize the faults within.

We need to ask ourselves honestly: Am I prepared to be free from all the false beliefs that have accumulated over this lifetime? If the answer is yes, then we need to give up our complaints and look within.

Discover how and in which relationships you have been creating suffering for yourself and others. Inquire into your own thoughts honestly, in a new manner. Use every complaint to look within and achieve clarity. Instead of working on changing others, we need to work on changing ourselves.

Once you focus inward and work on your shortcomings, the world will not appear the same. Gradually, you will begin to realize that this world is a marvelous system that resonates with your nature. It will begin to look more beautiful to you. You will be able to forgive people without complaining about them.

The day you find everyone beautiful and start liking everyone will be the day you have become a beautiful person. You will have learned to see the Source functioning through every human being. And then the world around you will change!

18

Law of Abundance

Overcome limitations with free flow

There were five brothers belonging to a very poor family. Their father was a fuel station attendant whose job was to fuel the vehicles that lined up at the station. The father led a miserable life, always grumbling, "Why am I so poor? When will my misery end?" He died a miserable death.

The five boys were all offered jobs at the fuel station so that they could support their family. They were paid a pittance individually –much less, than their father used to make, but collectively they were making a little more than their father. This is what happened to each of the five brothers:

The eldest brother always felt that they were being swindled. He remained poor his entire life. The second brother thought a little differently, though. "One day," he continued to say to himself, "I'll own a swanky car. But when will the struggle end?" He became moderately successful and managed to own a car after many years of struggle.

The third brother's focus was on more than owning just a car. He wanted to own a fuel station. "It will take some time, but that's okay," he continued to say to himself. Within a few years, he not only owned many cars but also a fuel station.

The fourth brother was the most ambitious. His focus was on smooth and massive success. His thoughts were, "This fuel must be arriving from somewhere. I want to be the owner of the source of all that fuel, soon." Within a brief period, because of his deep desire, he became the owner of an oil refinery.

The fifth brother, though, was the wisest. His focus was not on material possessions. He looked for the source of it all! His thoughts were, "What is the secret of life? There must be some reason why some people are poor and others aren't? What is the lesson my father never learned? Why do some people driving in expensive cars seem miserable in spite of their luxuries, and why do some without those luxuries seem so cheerful? I want to learn to be happy."

This brother met a number of wise men first at the fuel station and then at various other places. He started working for a wise man and became a great teacher himself. While he had access to all the riches of life —he chose to use his wealth and knowledge in the service of others, having understood the secrets of life.

All five brothers were presented with the same opportunity. Abundance, Wisdom, and Happiness were flowing their way. Each one attained these to the extent of the intensity of their desire, their direction of focus, and to the extent that their negative thoughts didn't block their progress.

The reason why many are focused on problems is because of their belief in scarcity and the need for struggle.

Many people believe in scarcity and entertain a feeling of 'lack'. Such a belief leads to competition and an unconscious notion that you have to take away from others in order to get something. Most corporate organizations and their marketing strategies are based on the approach of increasing the market share in a limited buyers' market. If wars between nations weren't enough, we now have corporate wars!

The universe is teeming with unlimited possibilities! The world in which we live is wonderfully obliging. The supreme creative potential of the Source makes it possible to fulfill the wishes of everyone simultaneously.

Allow 'faith in abundance' rather than 'fear of scarcity' to steer your life.

It's not easy at first to see abundance if you're used to seeing lack. But think about it —whenever there is a need (for energy, as an example) mankind has always come up with a solution. Innovators tap into the Source, for answers to problems. Otherwise, nuclear energy, solar energy, or any kind of energy that does not rely on fire, would not have been discovered and harnessed.

The point is there was a need for energy, and while those who believed in scarcity started hoarding and controlling wood, coal and oil, others–who did not have such a mindset of scarcity –found alternatives and learned how to harness renewable resources such as wind and solar energy.

The same principle works for any other need. Learn to see abundance rather than scarcity. You can choose to let creation happen in abundance rather than compete for a limited supply.

Learn to see the hidden truth of abundance of the Source instead of getting entangled in the illusion of scarcity. Learn to see that everything in the world is created in abundance. That's right! Everything you could possibly need or want has already been created for you. It's already in your life as in everyone's. In fact, everybody already has plenty of everything, regardless of the present appearance of their lives.

The Law of Abundance simply states:

There is abundance of everything for everyone.

Notice that there are no exceptions placed anywhere in this statement. There is abundance of love, peace, bliss, health and wealth in your life and also everyone's life. There is a natural flow of money, time, happiness, and harmony in your life and everyone's life.

The Divine Order of the Universe

You naturally progress toward your higher potential in life, so long as you do not place obstacles in the free-flow from the Source. This is the divine order of the universe.

The Divine Order is merely the law of nature that everything is in abundance. 'Divine' does not signify a particular God sitting in heaven and choosing if something should happen or not. It signifies the infinite possibilities that can unfold in your life by natural design.

Success is simple and natural and not the elusive element, many consider it to be. The only thing you must do is to allow it to unfold naturally. If you're not placing negative blocks in the flow of life, you'll automatically progress towards the higher aspects of life.

Your next question may be, "If this is true, then why do we see so much poverty and misery on Earth? Why isn't everyone experiencing abundance?" The secret again lies in your thoughts. If a child, born into a poor family, harbours no negative thoughts, he will automatically progress toward prosperity and abundance. Even if his focus is only a little more positive than negative, he will attract the best things in life. This is one of the reasons there are so many "rags-to-riches" stories.

Impoverished individuals, though, instead of thinking positively can't help but think of poverty. They do not realize that it is their thoughts that are poor. They despise and resist their impoverished living. Whatever they resist persists. For this reason, it can be said that the poor get poorer while the rich get richer.

Imagine every human being as being connected to the Universe through a pipe. Through that pipe, everything he needs is flowing to him –health, wealth, love, joy, prosperity and everything else he can conceive. Then, a negative thought enters his mind. It could even be a doubt about his wellbeing or a notion of scarcity. When he entertains a negative thought, or self-doubt, he is, in effect, placing a pebble in that pipeline. That pebble disrupts the flow of abundance. While one negative thought may not completely clog the pipeline, it does slow it to some extent. Should he continue to think more of such thoughts, you can imagine that soon the pebbles will be clogging more of the flow. With enough negative thinking, it wouldn't take long before the pebbles turn into rocks stopping that natural flow of bounty.

If you don't think a single negative thought, that's enough. You'll automatically be propelled towards physical vitality, mental growth, social harmony, financial abundance, and spiritual clarity that is readily available at the Source. This is the Divine Order of the Universe. But since man thinks negatively, he needs to ensure that his focus is on the positive and not the negative.

If we are not experiencing abundance in any one facet of our life, be it physical, mental, social, financial, or spiritual, it is because the free flow of abundance from the Source has been choked by limiting core thoughts, self-defeating core beliefs. For example, one of the core beliefs that most people live by is that they do not deserve good things in life. This belief chokes the free flow of abundance in all facets of their lives.

Another core belief that many people hold is to quantify abundance in terms of time and money. Time and money are merely means to an end. They are not the end in themselves! Therefore, our focus needs to be trained on what time and money can deliver us, rather than being stuck in the endless cycle of acquiring more time and money. We need to be focused on the quality of our life experiences rather than the quantity of money or time at our disposal.

Source Versus Force

This Law of Abundance can be also called the Law of Free Flow. Those who do not understand the Law of Abundance continue to exert their efforts forcefully to create what they aspire for.

When you are not connected with the Source, then you try to manifest your aspirations by force. You do not operate from the graceful state of free flow that is waiting to happen from the Source as per your divine plan. Such forceful efforts only produce limited results.

Any vibration that is forcefully generated dissolves with the passage of time. Such vibrations that are created by force are not enough to sustain the creative process and bring the manifestation into the visible realm of your life. Even if it does manifest, the results are not in harmony with the purpose of the Source and hence, it does not provide lasting fulfillment.

If you wish to attain your ultimate potential, then the creative vibration of thought needs to align with the ultimate purpose of the Source. People apply efforts to create a perfect life, however in doing so, they fall prey to the limiting situations that challenge them. They entertain negative feelings under the influence of scenes that delude them.

When certain events seem to go against what they desire, they conclude that they cannot attain fulfillment. When things don't seem to be going as planned, doubts arise. These very doubts bring down the vibration that would have manifested one's aspiration. All these thoughts of doubt are merely imaginary, focused on what "might" go wrong.

From the moment you wake up in the morning, you initiate vibrations through the thoughts that you entertain. These vibrations are the seeds of creation. If they are negative, they will manifest negativity. If they are positive, they will manifest positivity.

What will the vibration of assured abundance create? You will find that everything is already available to be experienced. Life will then abound in the feeling of gratitude.

But when unaware of this law, one believes that he will need to apply more force to manifest something. He tries brute force by exercising his will power. He tries to pull strings, use his connections with the seats of power to get his things done. He tries to acquire more information in his frenzy to manifest what he wishes. He tries to apply more effort in his haste to achieve his aspiration. Such a state of mind arises from ignorance –from the belief that it is only by 'doing' that one can achieve one's desires.

True creation from the Source does not happen that way.

Are you using forceful efforts backed by will power? Are you in a state of struggle? The results with this approach will not be sustainable. Certain things do get created with such forceful effort. However, when people believe that 'forceful doing' is the only way to achieve success, they see it as the only workable method and indulge in fierce competition due to the notion of scarcity. The notion of scarcity manifests only more scarcity.

The other method of creating is to be present with faith in the Law of Free-flow. You can bring forth the best things in your life by working with a deep assurance that there is enough of everything for everyone. The Law of Creation has already shown how you can bring forth the quality of the Source whenever and wherever you want.

When you look at everything you have as evidence of the free flow of the Source, your focus is on abundance and not on scarcity. Abundance then begins to assert itself in your life. The method of creating from the Source allows for the flow of abundance through you.

When you have unwavering faith in the Source and you live with a trust that everything is flowing in your life is from the Source, then you become receptive to abundance.

Thus, you solve problems with a deep assurance of abundance without worrying about any scarcity - of resources, of ideas, of time, of connections. The deep belief that everything is in abundance can create miracles in your life. In fact, with such a belief you will say there are no problems.

The only problem in life is to see circumstances as problems rather than opportunities.

When you truly experience the Source, you will cease to see the world as one with obstacles. You will tap into the fountainhead of abundance.

In the previous chapter, we looked at how the world is not really an obstacle; it is just a reflection of how you are. In this chapter, we looked at how circumstances and resources are not impediments. In the next chapter, we will discover whether people and their thoughts can pose hurdles.

19

Law of Influence
Circumvent others' thoughts

A man bought a little calf from the market. He put it on his shoulders and started walking back to his village. Three swindlers saw him and made a plan to cheat him out of that animal.

The first approached the man and said, "Why are you carrying a dog on your shoulders?" "This isn't a dog, it's a calf," the man said. "Since when have you started calling a dog a calf?!" said the swindler and walked away chuckling. The man shook his head and proceeded.

In a few minutes, he came across the second swindler, who said the same thing to him. This time, though, a doubt arose in the man's mind and he put the calf down.

Then the third swindler came along and inquired about his "dog." The man looked at his calf and then at the con man and screamed, "Yes, I have bought a dog to guard my house. Do you have a problem with that?!" The fraudster secretly smiled and left.

Now the man started thinking, "Have I actually been cheated into buying a dog instead of a calf? If my villagers come to know about this, they're going to make fun of me." He continued to think of this and allowed the calf to go, and quietly proceeded toward his home. The three swindlers laughed and walked away with the calf.

The swindlers planted the seed of doubt in this man's mind, "This isn't a calf, but a dog." And he received this idea from three different people. When the first person told him, he didn't believe it. When the second person repeated it, he began to have his doubts about what he truly believed and put the calf down. When the third person said the same thing, his thought turned to speech and he said, "Yes, I have bought a dog to guard my house."

These words reinforced his thought. He began imagining how the villagers would laugh at him when he came home with a dog instead of a calf. The thought turned to action and he let the calf go, convinced that it was a dog.

This is what exactly happens in our lives. The media, teachers, priests, parents, friends, etc. are all giving us their thoughts (which are their opinions, their versions of the truth). Thoughts are not just being given, but imposed upon us in such a manner that we don't have any doubts about their reality because they come from a popular reliable source. As a result, we believe those to be true. Our words and our actions, therefore follow, in blind faith.

In the social ecosystem which we live in, our lives are also driven by our interplay with people around us. Very often, people are held by the belief that their lives are largely determined by the choices of others around them.

Can your life be influenced by the thoughts of others? Do the choices of others affect you?

Many times, we feel that others are becoming obstacles in our expression. Most people tend to squarely blame people around them for situations in their lives. You would have heard people saying, "If only this person were to change, all my problems will vanish". Perhaps you would at times, have thought this way.

Is it really possible to be insulated from the world in a way that others' thoughts do not influence us?

The Law of Influence has the answer to all these questions. It states:

> ***People's thoughts cannot influence you,***
> ***unless you allow them to.***

Children are particularly vulnerable to others' thoughts as their power of discretion is not developed to be able to make choices. They are affected because they are dependent on others such as their parents. They need parental guidance, and so they automatically believe anything the parents tell them, either through words, actions or thoughts.

If a baby is in the womb and the mother thinks negatively, then it has a negative impact on the unborn baby. Babies are simple beings; they're sculpted as you mould them. At this point, the baby is a part of the mother's body. Diseases, harmful qualities and habits of the mother can be imbibed by the baby while in the womb. In the same manner, positive thoughts and beliefs are also impregnated in the foetus, much before birth.

When you grow up, the thoughts of others stop having a *direct* influence upon you. It's simply not possible that someone who prays for you to fall sick could actually make you sick. The only way for someone else to impact you is if you begin to think the same negative thoughts.

For example, suppose you break apart from someone and the person curses you that your life will become a wreck. If you agree with that statement at a subconscious level, then those words will affect you. But if you choose not to believe those words, they will have no effect on you.

If someone staying with you is a negative thinker, then his negative thinking will not affect you as long as you maintain your vigilance. For instance, if you're alert while giving them a ride in your car, then their negative thinking won't cause you to have an accident.

Let's say, though, they're constantly saying negative things while they're riding with you: "The number of accidents has increased alarmingly. Yesterday, there was a terrible accident on this highway. The other day, I witnessed a gruesome accident. You should drive carefully!"These negative words may begin to affect you, causing you to start thinking in a similar negative manner. You then may begin to attract an accident as a result. But be assured that if you don't allow yourself to be influenced by them, you will not encounter an accident.

You would have heard people say, "We're suffering the karmic effects of others' deeds. All these incidents are happening to us because of others' karma." If you unconsciously hold on to such thinking, then these beliefs indirectly affect your present condition. Do not allow the mindset of people living with you to negatively influence your thoughts. If you deliberately and consciously don't let this happen, you won't experience any negative effects.

The truth of the matter is that there are negative thinkers present on every bus and every train in every city of the world. But their thoughts have no significance on whether the vehicle is involved in an accident or arrives safely at its destination. Only the thoughts of the driver of the vehicle play any significant role in the safety of the ride. If there are some negative thinkers travelling with you, there is no reason to be worried.

You should care about your own thinking as it is the only thing in your control. You should ask yourself, "How are my thoughts?" If you discover that you, too, are having thoughts of an impending accident, reassure yourself by saying, "The driver's thoughts are positive. So I need not worry." This nullifies the impact of your negative thinking. As long as the driver doesn't allow the negative thoughts of the passengers to affect his thoughts, the journey will conclude without a hitch.

Just imagine if the thoughts of all the negative thinkers on these vehicles actually had an effect on the driver, then how many buses or trains do you think would reach their destination safely and on time? It's good that only the thinking of the driver is what counts.

Similarly, you are the 'driver' of your life and your thoughts are the driving force. If you understand the Laws of Thought, then you won't face any trouble even if you interact with negative people. Be aware and be vigilant to avoid being swayed when you're listening to their negative chatter. The only influential factor in your life is *your* own thoughts.

Here is another example of how the Law of Influence operates:

> Two teams are in the midst of a crucial football match with thousands of spectators watching. Obviously, there are jumbled collective thoughts, not only in the minds of the spectators, but in those of the players as well.

> The thoughts in the players' minds change with each successful move by the opposite team. They begin to think that they might lose the game and this impacts their game. The match ends by one team beating the other by 4 to 3 - a difference of just one goal.

> The thoughts of millions of spectators being expressed in the form of clapping or hooting may very well affect the morale of the players, but the ultimate deciding factor in the game is the thoughts going through the minds of the players on the field.

How Do Your Thoughts Influence Others?

This law also begs the question: Can you help other people through your own personal thoughts? If you pray for them, will it help them?

When you pray for someone, your thoughts influence that person's life only to the extent that he or she is receptive to it. When you're trying to heal someone, the beliefs of the person being healed are still the most relevant. At the very least, you must stop saying negative things about others, lest you influence their thinking. This is where the power of words becomes apparent. Be careful with the words you say to yourself and to others.

You probably unknowingly utter some negative sentences every day. This depletes the power of your words. You can increase the power of your words by consciously choosing positive words. Instead of saying, "Don't scream," you can say, "Speak softly." Instead of saying, "Don't stress about it", you can say, "Relax."

Just the understanding that people's thoughts cannot influence you until you allow, is enough to insulate you from the negativities of the world. However, if someone is speaking negatively around you and you want to be sure that such a thought does not even make an iota of impact on you, you may meditate to access the Source.

Dip into the Source using any of the methods outlined in the first section of the book and you will automatically feel peaceful and in harmony with the universe. In such a state, no negative thought can impact you.

There is a golden rule that can work wonders. Always believe what your inner experience is telling you rather than the opinion of others. This experience speaks to you and becomes audible and clear when you access the Source.

When you connect with the Presence and communicate with others, you will find that people respond to you positively, instead of reacting mechanically.

Does this mean that your thoughts are influencing them? No. It is not about your thoughts. When you are connected to the Source whilst communicating with the world, you touch the same life source within the people around you. People become receptive to those who are brimming with love, joy and peace of the Source.

20

Law of Integrity
Connecting the dots

The one who walks his talk,
His feet are worthy of worship.
~A couplet by Saint Tukaram

The first six laws are incomplete without the seventh one. This law integrates the others. The missing piece in the jigsaw puzzle of how to create from the Source is integrity.

Integrity has to do with aligning your words and actions with your thoughts and feelings. Your feelings and thoughts are reflected in your words and actions. It can't help but be any other way. When your thoughts and feelings are aligned in the direction of what you aspire for, your words and actions have to follow.

For example, a person will be penalized for stealing, he cannot escape being penalized simply by saying he doesn't want to be punished. The punishment is the result of his stealing.

To change the results of actions, you'll have to change what you're doing –the actions themselves. In order to change what you're doing, your thoughts and feelings must change.

The Law of Integrity strings together all the other Laws of Thought. It simply states:

Align your feelings, thoughts, words and actions to achieve your highest potential.

Thoughts, feelings, words, and actions all manifest within the Source –within your *witnessing presence*. Thus, the four aspects of thinking, feeling, speech, and action arise from and exist within your *being*. These aspects, as you see, have to be in alignment for you to achieve your highest potential.

If you are not progressing in any area of your life, then at least one of these aspects isn't in tune with the others. You may want something and you're thinking positively about it, but you're feeling negative about it. One day, you may feel and think positively, but then the next day you may say negative words about what you want to create. You may even find that there are days when your actions reflect the exact opposite of what you're thinking and saying.

Another way to understand the importance of the integrity of these elements is to understand the link between them:

- Thoughts and feelings *arise* from the Source, in the field of consciousness.

- Everything is *designed* on the thought plane first and *powered* by feelings.

- Thoughts and feelings *affect* your words and actions.

- Your actions *result* in consequences.

Integrity of thoughts, feelings, words, and actions is critical because they are all inevitably connected.

Developing this integrity is vital to reaching your highest potential. The more you are aware of your thoughts, feelings, words and actions, the more they will be aligned. Let's explore how you can achieve this consistently in order to create desired results as quickly as possible.

Be Keenly Aware of Your Thoughts

There are circumstances in life where many of us feel unworthy and tell ourselves, "I don't deserve this." You cannot underestimate the extent of the damage that you could inflict on yourself simply by uttering this sentence to yourself.

The mind replays this particular thought, adopts it, and provides us with situations in our lives to prove that we are, indeed, unworthy. We would then start doing things to appear unworthy to ourselves. Though this may sound absurd, such is the power of the mind. There is no limit to what the mind can bring about, out of ignorance and lack of awareness.

When it comes to what you aspire for, be aware of exactly what you're telling your mind.

> A lady who wanted to become a doctor repeatedly visualized herself checking the blood pressure of patients, dressing their wounds, and otherwise taking care of others. She became a nurse.

It's vital you stay cognizant of your thoughts. If there is one thing about your thoughts to be vigilant of, it's the rule:

You must never trust your thoughts when you are in sorrow or when your consciousness is low.

Decisions made in times of distress, often prove to be wrong. Additionally, you'll be amazed at the great number of flawed thoughts that continually pour in when you're feeling depressed or frustrated. This is exactly when it's imperative to apply the rule. Tell yourself, "*I must not trust these thoughts at this point in time; they aren't reliable.*"

You must remind yourself of this rule whenever you are in deep sorrow and when thoughts like, "Don't talk to that person anymore", "You ought to teach them a lesson", or "Nobody can be trusted" invade your mind. Decisions you make when you're in that state of mind will often turn out to be wrong. Instead, tell yourself, "I should not trust these thoughts. I should listen, instead, to a discourse on Truth; I should read something about Truth and contemplate on it; I should practice meditation." Applying this rule in times of grief, stress, anger, or fear, helps you avoid the downward spiral of negativity.

As you apply this important rule, you begin to recognize how untrustworthy your mind is when you're not thinking positive thoughts. But more than that, you'll also come to realize how trustworthy your decisions are when you're happy. A happy person never wants to hurt anyone else. They are truthful and abide in the Source.

Be Vigilant About Your Feelings

Always be vigilant about the feelings you hold for your intended aspirations. Take a pause occasionally to examine whether you have any unconscious negative feelings about the situation. Clear your feelings if there is any residual resistance. Clear any negative feelings that you experience by re-affirming their positive equivalents.

For example, if you feel gripped with fear then re-affirm, "Though this feeling of fear is present, I am fully in favour of Faith and Courage." If you feel consumed by hatred, then re-affirm, "Though hatred is being felt, I am fully in favour of love and compassion."

Some negative feelings and their positive equivalents are given below:

Feeling	In favour of...
Anger	Love, Joy, Peace
Boredom	Enthusiasm
Comparison	Evenness
Depression	Bliss, Wonder, Joy
Ego	Witnessing Presence, Humility
Fear	Faith, Courage
Greed	Contentment
Hatred	Love, Compassion
Ill-will	Benevolence, Goodwill
Jealousy	Equanimity, Evenness

When you desire something, it is enough to tell your subconscious mind that you are in need of a job. It will work toward realizing your desire. You only need to communicate the "what" and not the "how" of anything you desire. People tend to worry about "how" the process will follow, which merely brings up the wrong feelings within them.

All you need to is to decide the result and let go of the worry of how to achieve it. Leave that to your subconscious mind. Its job is to match your outer reality to your inner reality. Let your subconscious mind come up with the right situations and guide you in the right actions to manifest your aspirations.

Be Attentive to the Words You Speak or Hear

Remember as you go about your day, to keep your words positive regarding your desired result; appreciate all positive words that you hear about your aspiration. Additionally, take care that you are not saying anything negative regarding your abilities or the situation. Be careful not to utter words that would work against achieving your desired goal.

> A group of frogs decided to hold a friendly race. One frog, in particular, took a stunning lead and eventually leapt ahead of all the rest, winning the race with ease. The other frogs, instead of running the race, were conversing about the difficulties that they would face and the dangers they would encounter in the competition. Because of all this talk, these frogs actually were so fearful of losing the race that they were hesitant to even take a step forward.

While all the other frogs were engrossed in the conversation, the frog which eventually won the contest had already started his way up. Even as the other frogs called out to him, trying to warn him of the dangers ahead, he kept moving steadily up and achieved his goal. It turned out that the frog which won was deaf; he couldn't hear the negative conversation.

We must learn to become like that frog: deaf to anything negative. Turn a deaf ear to negative statements like: "It's not possible, people are bad, the world isn't a safe place, nothing good will happen," and other such negative statements. As people read newspapers and watch the news, it's easy to see how they can get swept in the spiral of negativity and say, "Politicians will never change; corruption will remain; war is inevitable; people are bad."

Little do they understand that they are misusing their verbal power by repeating negative words and attracting negativity into their lives. Many people tend to espouse negative energy without even thinking about it. You must not allow their words to affect you. You need to be attentive for this.

Be Mindful of Your Actions

When you firmly believe your desires will be fulfilled, let your actions demonstrate only your positive intentions regarding your goal. Exercise your faith by performing an action as if the desire were already fulfilled. For example, if your goal is to own a certain make and model of car, then buy a keychain that has the insignia of that car on it. This is termed as "Faith in Action."

Take steps, even small ones, towards your desired result. If you want to lose weight, clean out your refrigerator of all junk food. You could even buy clothes of a slimmer fit. After all, you will need them once you lose weight! If you want to pass an examination at the end of the year, buy the books for the next year's course. These are examples of Faith in Action.

Be aware that your actions demonstrate faith and not mistrust or doubt about your goal. It's your job to imagine… believe… expect… and to take inspired action, but it is not your job to orchestrate the manifestation of your desires!

'*Being aware*' is the common denominator to these four aspects. How do we raise our awareness toward our thoughts, feelings, words and actions? There are many ways:

People are predominantly either visual, or auditory or kinesthetic in the way they understand and deal with inputs. Those who are visual, see things in their minds. They see concepts as images. Their mental imagery is very vivid. That is their predominant way to think and process information. Those who are auditory hear sounds or words in their heads. They are more attuned to words. Those who are kinesthetic are more oriented towards their feelings and sensations. They get feelings about their surroundings and are sensitive to environmental perceptions.

When you raise your awareness of all of these –thought, feelings, words, and actions– you're becoming aware of how you process information. At a minimum, you need to be aware of the predominant way you process information.

As your awareness rises, your mind will automatically begin waving a red flag when any thought or feeling that is not positive appears. Your mind will immediately tell you, "The thought appearing now is not reliable." Your negative feelings will serve as reminders for the positive feelings that you choose to experience. Bringing integrity in your thoughts, feelings, words and actions will keep you from making wrong decisions.

When we bring integrity into our lives, we move from leading a fragmented way of life into wholesome existence. This makes it natural and simple to access and abide in the experience of the Source, and to express its divine qualities.

Epilogue

Of the seeds that are scattered on earth, how many successfully sprout and grow to their fullest potential? Not all. Only a few get the right soil. But not all such seeds get sufficient water at the right time. Among the ones that do, not all of them receive adequate sunlight, shade, or nourishment. Among the few that get all of these, some may be trampled by cattle. Thus, some deficiency causes the seed to not grow to its fullest potential.

If all the necessities were fulfilled, would the seed still flourish? The seed needs to sacrifice itself for the sapling to take birth. It has to allow its walls to dissolve and merge into the surrounding soil, so that it gives way to the sapling. The purpose of the seed is fulfilled only through its sacrifice, its willingness to dedicate itself to transformation. It is like the caterpillar that undergoes metamorphosis only when it sacrifices itself to go through the stage of the cocoon and then strives out of it. Only then does the butterfly emerge and take flight in all its glory.

The wisdom of the Source and the powers and laws that serve to experience and create from the Source represent nourishment that the caterpillar gathers, that helps it on its journey ahead.

Having gathered and assimilated these laws and powers, we need to apply them in our daily life. Whilst applying them, we need to contemplate upon the lessons that we gather in everyday life.

The caterpillar dedicates itself to the stage of the cocoon. The cocoon in the caterpillar's journey of metamorphosis represents the period where we commit ourselves to transformation by applying and experimenting with these laws and powers.

When the would-be butterfly strives to come out of the cocoon, it applies pressure on the cocoon walls with its unformed wings. This striving actually helps strengthen its wings. Those caterpillars that do not apply their energies remain stuck inside the cocoon. This striving to break out of the cocoon represents the ultimate human challenge of getting out of the shell of our old identity that was built on limiting beliefs, to realize our fullest potential.

When we limit ourselves to our comfort-zone and resist or shy away from the struggles of life, we remain like seeds that never blossom to the fullest. The seed has the potential of becoming a full grown tree and ultimately an entire forest! If the seed falls short of this, it feels incomplete that 'I could not become what I was meant to be. I could not fulfill what I was destined for.'

Just as the caterpillar realizes the purpose of struggling out of the cocoon only after it emerges, it is only after going through challenging situations in life that we realize that they were opportunities meant for us to explore and experiment, so as to realize our highest creative potential.

Any transformation in life requires the investment of time, attention and effort. If you are committed to work, so as to allow the Source to manifest in your life, it is recommended that you take a short break from your daily routine. You may take three to four days off from work, if that's easily possible.

Commit yourself to reflect on your life. Create your own personal action plan to ingrain the practices of meditation into your routine. Consider how the Laws of Thought have been functioning in your life and chart out how you plan to create your future.

If it is possible, you may consider attending the Magic of Ultimate Awakening Retreat (details are provided in the pages that follow). In this retreat, you can experientially learn how to live from pure presence, allowing the qualities of the Source to manifest. You will learn practical tools to quiet the chattering mind and access pure consciousness at will. The retreat provides the path to shift from mind-centered living to consciousness-centered living.

There are no coincidences in this universe. Everything in the universe happens in perfect order, and this wisdom reaching each one of us is no exception. We can feel gratitude for this, for the more we feel it, the more it begins to work in our lives. Being in this feeling of gratitude is indeed a celebration of life.

Let an earnest thirst emerge within us to realize our fullest potential. May our life be driven by the highest purpose of the Source, propelling us to enact our divine plan, fulfilling our life purpose of being the Source!

You can send your opinion or feedback on this book to:
Tej Gyan Foundation, P.O. Box 25, Pimpri Colony,
Pimpri, Pune – 411017, Maharashtra, INDIA
Email: englishbooks@tejgyan.org

Write for Us

We welcome writers, translators and editors to join our team. If you would like to volunteer, please email us at: englishbooks@tejgyan.org or call : +91 90110 10963

APPENDIX

About Sirshree

Sirshree's spiritual quest, which began during his childhood, led him on a journey through various schools of thought and prevalent meditation practices. His overpowering desire to attain the Truth made him relinquish his teaching profession. After a long period of contemplation on the truth of life, his spiritual quest culminated in the attainment of the ultimate truth. Since then, over the last two decades, he has dedicated his life toward elevating mass consciousness and making spiritual pursuit simple and accessible to all.

Sirshree espouses, **"All paths that lead to the truth begin differently, but culminate at the same point – understanding. Understanding is complete in itself. Listening to this understanding is enough to attain the truth."**

Sirshree has delivered more than 3000 discourses that throw light on this understanding, simplify various aspects of life and unravel missing links in spirituality. He delivers the understanding in casual contemporary language by weaving profound aspects into analogies, parables and humor that provoke one to contemplate.

To make it possible for people from all walks of life to directly experience this understanding, Sirshree has designed the *Maha Aasmani Param Gyan Shivir* – a retreat designed as a comprehensive system for imparting wisdom. This system for wisdom, which has been accredited with ISO 9001:2015 certification, has inspired thousands of seekers from all walks of life to progress on their journey of the Truth. This system makes the wisdom accessible to every human being, regardless of religion, caste, social strata, country or belief system.

Sirshree is the founder of Tej Gyan Foundation, a no-profit organization committed to raising mass consciousness with branches in India, the United States, Europe and Asia-Pacific. Sirshree's retreats have transformed the lives of thousands and his teachings have inspired various social initiatives for raising global consciousness.

His published work includes more than 100 books, some of which have been translated in more than 10 languages and published by leading publishers. Sirshree's books provide profound and practical reading on existential subjects like emotional maturity, harmony in relationships, developing self-belief, overcoming stress and anxiety, and dealing with the question of life-beyond-death, to name a few. His literature on core spirituality expounds the deeper meaning of self-realization and self-stabilization, unravelling missing links in the understanding of karma, wisdom, devotion, meditation and consciousness.

Various luminaries and celebrities like His Holiness the Dalai Lama, publishers Mr. Reid Tracy, Ms. Tami Simon and Yoga Master Dr. B. K. S. Iyengar have released Sirshree's books and lauded his work. "The Source" book series, authored by Sirshree, has sold over 10 million copies in 5 years. His book, "The Warrior's Mirror", published by Penguin, was featured in the Limca Book of Records for being released on the same day in 11 languages.

Tejgyan... The Road Ahead
What is Tejgyan?

Tejgyan is the wisdom of the existential truth, which is beyond duality. "Gyan" is a term commonly used for "knowledge". Tejgyan is the wisdom beyond knowledge and ignorance. It is understanding that arises from direct experience of the final truth. It is what sets us free from the limitations of the mind and opens us to our highest potential.

In today's world, there are people who feel disharmony and are desperately trying to achieve balance in an unpredictable life. Tejgyan helps them in harmonizing with their true nature, the Self, thereby restoring balance in all aspects of their lives.

And then, there are those who are successful, but feel a sense of emptiness within. Tejgyan provides them fulfilment and helps them to embark on a journey towards self-realization. There are others who feel lost and are seeking the meaning of life. Tejgyan helps them to realize the true purpose of human life.

All this is possible with Tejgyan due to a very simple reason. The experience of the ultimate truth (God or Pure consciousness) is always available. The direct experience of this truth is possible provided the right method is known. Tejgyan is that method, that understanding.

The understanding of Tejgyan makes it possible to lead a life of freedom from fear, worry, anger and stress. It helps in attaining physical vitality, emotional strength and stability, harmony in relationships, financial freedom and spiritual progress.

At Tej Gyan Foundation, Sirshree imparts this understanding through a System for Wisdom – a series of retreats that guides participants step by step towards realizing the true Self, being established in the experience of self-realization, and expressing its qualities. This system for wisdom has been accredited with the ISO 9001:2015 certification.

Maha Aasmani Param Gyan Shivir

"**Maha Aasmani Param Gyan Shivir**" is the flagship Self-realization retreat offered by Tej Gyan Foundation. The retreat is conducted in Hindi. The teachings of the retreat are non-denominational (secular).

This residential retreat is held for 3 to 5 days at the foundation's MaNaN Ashram amidst the glory of the mountains and the pristine beauty of nature. The Ashram is located at the outskirts of the city of Pune in India, and is well connected by air, road and rail. The retreat is also held at other centres of Tej Gyan Foundation across the world.

You can participate in this retreat to attain ageless wisdom through a unique System for Wisdom so that you can:

● Discover "Who am I" through direct experience.

● Learn to abide in pure consciousness while functioning in the world, allowing the qualities of consciousness like peace, love, joy, compassion, abundance and creativity to manifest.

● Acquire simple tools to use in everyday life, which help quiet the chattering mind.

● Get practical techniques to be in the present and connect to the source of all answers within (the inner guru).

● Discover missing links in the practices of Meditation (*Dhyana*), Action (*Karma*), Wisdom (*Gyana*) and Devotion (*Bhakti*).

- Understand the nature of your body-mind mechanism to attain freedom form its tendencies.

- Learn practical methods to shift from mind-centered living to consciousness-centered living.

A Mini-retreat is also conducted, especially for teenagers (14 to 16 years of age) during summer and winter vacations.

To register for retreats, visit www.tejgyan.org,

contact (+91) 9921008060, or email mail@tejgyan.com

About Tej Gyan Foundation

Tej Gyan Foundation (TGF) was established with the mission of creating a highly evolved society through all-round development of every individual that transforms all the facets of their lives. It is a non-profit organization, founded on the teachings of Sirshree.

The Foundation has received the ISO certification (ISO 9001:2015) for its system of imparting wisdom. It has centres all across India as well as in other countries. The motto of Tej Gyan Foundation is 'Happy Thoughts'.

At the core of the philosophy of Tejgyan is the Power of Acceptance. Acceptance has profound meaning and is at the core of our Being. It is Acceptance that brings forth true love, joy and peace.

Symbol of Acceptance

The Symbol of Acceptance – shown above – is a representation of this truth. The symbol represents brackets. Whatever occurs in life falls within these brackets that signify acceptance of whatever *is*. Hence, this symbol forms the centerpiece of the Foundation's MaNaN Ashram.

The Foundation is creating a highly evolved society through:

- ☐ Tejgyan Programs (Retreats, YouTube Webcasts)
- ☐ Tejgyan Books and Apps
- ☐ Tejgyan Projects (Value education, Women empowerment, Peace initiatives)

The Foundation undertakes projects to elevate the level of consciousness among students, youth, women, senior citizens, teachers, doctors, leaders, professionals, corporate and Government organizations, police force, prisoners etc.

the
$ource SERIES

For a Balanced Life

Read the Source series to attain a balanced life, comprising 3 key facets: Mastery of Mind, Physical Vitality and Fulfilment at Work.

The Source

Access the Source of Love, Joy and Peace

Discover the Source of creation within you... Realize the 7 Powers of the Source in daily life... Leverage the 7 Laws of Thought to achieve mastery of the mind.

The Source of Health

The Key to Perfect Health Discovery

Discover the connection between your mind and body and how they relate to consciousness. Learn 7 principles and 7 tools to transform your physical health.

The Source @ Work

A Story of Inspiration from Jeeodee

Understand the principles of natural communication and effortless productivity through a story. Enjoy, energize and elevate your work with cues from this story.

The Source Series of Pocket Books

To make the wisdom of The Source accessible to the masses, it has been presented in the form of 10 pocket books that deal with its application in various facets of life. Millions of these pocket books have been distributed to people from various walks of life through the Foundation's volunteers.

Other Related Books by Sirshree

The Third side of the Coin
Unraveling Missing Links in Spirituality

The Third side of the Coin is a way of life, beyond fixed views. It is an approach of openness that transcends the dualities of life. Living on the third side of the coin of life gives us insights about how life works.

This book explains the limitations of prevalent beliefs in the light of higher wisdom. It unravels deeper secrets in various facets of life—starting with aspects like prayer, problems, desires, destiny, rebirth, and then moving onto deeper spiritual realities.

ISBN:

978-81-8415-640-9

Total Pages: 200

WOW Publishings Pvt. Ltd.

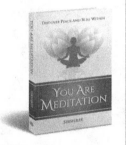

YOU ARE MEDITATION
Discover Peace and Bliss within

Starting with the basics, this book will guide you towards the ultimate goal of meditation where you dissolve into the silent stillness of pure consciousness and realize that you are meditation – your true nature of love, bliss and peace. The book demystifies meditation by examining both its superficial and its most profound benefits. It elaborates the training and practice needed to master the body–mind.

ISBN:

978-81-8322-786-5

Total Pages: 160

Manjul Publishing House Pvt.Ltd.

The Secret of Awakening

The Source of Answers is Within You

This book is a compilation of profound answers that arise from the quintessence of wisdom.

What is the purpose of human life? What is wrong with desiring the fruit of our actions? What is the purpose of relationships? Is it spiritually wrong to pursue and acquire money? If God exists, why can't we see him? If God is perfect, what was the need to create an imperfect world? How can I free myself from the clutches of my past?

The answers to these questions and more, asked by seekers of truth and answered by Sirshree, unravel the deepest truths of life, dissolving our dilemmas and revealing the essence of spirituality.

ISBN:

978-93-86618-27-6

Total Pages: 228

Pentagon Press

For further details contact:

Tejgyan Global Foundation

Registered Office: Happy Thoughts Building, Vikrant Complex, Near Tapovan Mandir, Pimpri, Pune 411017, Maharashtra, India.
Contact No: 020-27411240, 27412576
Email: mail@tejgyan.com
MaNaN Ashram: Survey No. 43, Sanas Nagar, Nandoshi gaon, Kirkatwadi Phata, Sinhagad Road, Tal. Haveli, Dist. Pune 411024, Maharashtra, India. Contact No: 992100 8060.

Hyderabad: 9885558100, **Bangalore:** 9880412588,
Delhi : 9891059875, **Nashik:** 9326967980, **Mumbai:** 9373440985

For accessing our unique 'System for Wisdom' from self-help to self-realization, please follow us on:

	Website Online Shopping/ Blog	www.tejgyan.org www.gethappythoughts.org
You Tube	Video Channel	www.youtube.com/tejgyan For Q&A videos: http://goo.gl/YA81DQ
facebook	Social networking	www.facebook.com/tejgyan
twitter	Social networking	www.twitter.com/sirshree
	Internet Radio	http://www.tejgyan.org/ internetradio.aspx

Pray for World Peace along with thousands of others every day at 09:09am and 09:09pm

Divine Light of Love, Bliss and Peace is Showering;
The Golden Light of Higher Consciousness is Rising;
All negativity on Earth is Dissolving;
Everyone is in Peace and Blissfully Shining;
O God, Gratitude for Everything!